Book 1/3: The Entrée

BE THE ONE
WHO WINS THE ONE FOR THE ONE

A Handbook on Soul Winning

ANDREW PURCHASE

Be The One
Andrew Purchase © 2025

wintheone.org

Published by Win The One Ltd
Printed by IngramSpark

ISBN: 978-1-7642207-0-5

Cover design in collaboration with Beckon Creative
Interior design & typeset by Beckon Creative
Frontispiece image used: Kevin Carden | Lightstock

 A catalogue record for this book is available from the National Library of Australia

BISAC Subjects: 1. Evangelism 2. Christian Living 3. Autobiography

The author asserts their moral right to be identified as the author of this work.

All rights reserved. No part of this publication may be reproduced, stored in a retrieval system, or transmitted in any form or by any means—electronic, mechanical, photocopying, recording, or otherwise—without prior written permission of the publisher, except in the case of brief quotations in critical articles or reviews.

Scripture quotations taken from the New King James Version®. Copyright © 1982 by Thomas Nelson. Used by permission. All rights reserved.

This book is published using Australian English spelling and conventions. Readers may notice differences in spelling and expressions compared to other forms of English; these reflect the author's use of Australian vernacular.

ENDORSEMENTS

ANDREW PURCHASE IS A RARE BREED! While the rest of us well-meaning, Jesus-loving Christians pluck up the courage to mumble to the shop attendant that God loves them, Andrew dives right in with Holy Spirit aplomb. Is it bravery? Foolhardy lack of self-consciousness? A gift of evangelism endowed on the few? I came to Christ because Andrew spoke words that made sense and also answered the questions I was secretly asking God. Did he have a private hotline to God? I have seen the pews of a church filled to overflowing with people from every conceivable walk of life who came to accept Christ after an encounter with Andrew. He was, and still is, tenacious, gentle and one-eyed in his desire to see the kingdom here on earth.

Andrew has a rare ability to articulate the complexities of the gospel so the simple can understand, the broken hear words of hope, the lost find forgiveness and the hardest of hearts are softened.

And now this compelling story of how to win souls for Jesus is recorded in black and white. It's not a mystery—it's a story about how the love for God and fellow humankind can drive one man to see amazing miracles of faith and salvation.

— *The Italian Catholic Hippie*

It only takes hours to read a book, but in this case, a lifetime to write one. For many years I have witnessed Andrew connect with and win people into the Kingdom and go on to see them live for God. Not just through a gifting, but through practical insights and understanding.

Like a master craftsman he shares these insights through wonderful real conversion stories and then lays out practical wisdom that can be learnt by all who seek to be effective soul-winners. Of all our pursuits, surely this is worthy of our attention.

Over 40 years Andrew has been the most fruitful soul-winner I have seen. I believe this handbook will be a great blessing to many who have a heart to see people brought to Jesus but are daunted and unsure how to start, and an equally wonderful blessing to those who wish to be more effective in their witness for Jesus. An invitation to adventure.

— *PV Master Builder*

DEDICATION

I WOULD LIKE TO THANK Visser and like-minded friends who have walked the journey with me, for without their quality friendship I could not have fulfilled the purposes of God.

> *... But there is a friend who sticks closer than a brother.*
> Proverbs 18:24

To my beloved wife, Haidie, whose love and kindness, sense of humour and profound walk with God, as well as her editing skills, have undergirded this book and my life. For her, I am extremely grateful.

> *... her worth is far above rubies.*
> Proverbs 31:10

And finally, *Be the One, Who Wins the One, For The One* would not have eventuated without those hardy souls who ventured from the comfort of their churches to find me and challenge me to seek Christ. Their bold moves rescued me from the clutches of hell and a life in a wheelchair. Without them I would not have found the truth, deliverance or healing, and the many, many hundreds of souls who have found Christ since.

*And how shall they preach
unless they are sent?*

*As it is written: 'How beautiful are the feet
of those who preach the gospel of peace, who
bring glad tidings of good things!'*

Romans 10:15

CONTENTS

Introduction		11
PART ONE		**17**
Story:	The Ice Man	19
Tool:	The Baby on the Bin	26
Story:	The Ice Man, Continued	33
Tool:	Meeting your Future Spouse and Striking Gold	37
Story:	The Psychiatrist	41
Tool:	The Seed Must Go In	46
Story:	The Feral Surfers	51
Tool:	The Umbilical Cord of Life	56
Tool:	Why is the baby nine months in the womb?	60
Story:	The Dux of the School	67
Tool:	Love and Respect	71
Story:	The Handsome Lonely Surfer	75
Tool:	Prayer works	81
Story:	Popeye, The Scandinavian Viking	87
Tool:	Don't waste six months	91
Story:	Mad Thommo and The Scary Bikie	95
Tool:	Not Interested in Church but Open to Jesus	100
Story:	The Leading Hand	103
Tool:	'Paul Plants and Apollos Waters' in Context	109

PART TWO 113

My Story		115
Tool:	Understanding Appropriate Responses	124
Tool:	Appropriate Responses in Soul-winning	128
My Story:	The Exodus	131
Tool:	Inappropriate Responses in Soul-winning	139
My Story:	The Way, The Truth and The Life	143
Tool:	The Importance of Sending	150
My Story:	The Finger of God	155
Tool:	Jesus Was Not Only Sent, but He Sends	159
My Story:	The Word, Part One	165
Tool:	The Power of One	169
My Story:	The Word, Part Two	175
Tool:	Beachheads	179
My Story:	Healed	185

PART THREE 193

Story:	My Best Friend	195
Tool:	Unbelievable Converts: Don't Judge a Book by its Cover	200
Tool:	Unbelievable Converts: Overcoming Intimidation	206
Story:	The Handsome Ladies' Man & The Angry Man with the Wild Hair	213

Tool:	Getting on the Same Page with Key Definitions	217
Story:	The Shy Guy	223
Tool:	The Napkin Diagram	229
Story:	The Italian Catholic Hippie	235
Tool:	Same But Different	239

Final Thoughts	245
About the Author	249

INTRODUCTION

WELCOME TO *BE THE ONE*.

Be the One, Who Wins the One, For the One has grown into three books, kind of like a trilogy, but more importantly a body of work. It's primarily a body of work because it took many years to unpack the processes I learnt in winning souls. These precious souls were not just won, but saved in such a way that they grew into leaders and won their own friends and family to Christ. This has been a powerful journey of discovery with God who instructed me to share what I had learnt and to pass it on to those who are interested in winning souls.

This first book, *Be The One*, is a fresh and vital look at how to work with God and people. These are truths borne from years at the coal face. The book holds precious insights and powerful keys and while the stories are exciting, they are also instructional, because I want you to experience your own moves of God in your personal vineyards.

I've selected from my personal experiences a number of inspiring stories of souls won to Christ.

They come from all walks of life and backgrounds. But I have also provided reasons for *why* they were won, and called these 'tools' so you can add them to your own soul-winning toolbox.

This is a street-smart manual for winning souls written in a colloquial tone so anybody can relate. It is not a heavy theological thesis but a conversation. I want to inspire and galvanise the everyday believer into action in their local area, backed by sound doctrine and solid Biblical truths and insights.

Be The One, Who Wins the One, For The One is a body of work that, like Rome, was not built in a day, but more like a decade or two. It took a while. It took some time to understand the concepts and then build them into a frame work of practical tools easily understood. This was not an academic exercise but rather a working relationship with Holy Spirit; the process became more detailed as it progressed, and that's why it's important to take the time to read all three books.

It also took a while because I'm dyslexic. You can get away with this as a speaker—however, not so with writing. It is extremely unforgiving. I miss words, write the sentence backwards and struggle with grammar. Without dyslexia it would have taken a quarter of the time. For those with dyslexia, please be encouraged: while it's hard, it's still achievable to write, and the message/concepts/ideas you have to share will prevail. Thankfully my wife, an English Literature teacher, helped me re-write the manuscript numerous times;

but slowly my writing improved and morphed into something that was readable.

Lastly, in writing this book the battle was so fierce and there were a great number of personal setbacks that made daily writing difficult to accomplish. I know this fierce battle was to stop it getting written and published, because in the hands of soul-winners it could revolutionise individuals, churches, communities and the Kingdom of God. Nothing is as important to God as the saving of a soul, a lost sheep. Therefore everything has been against it being published.

My hope is that every believer would be inspired to win the lost sheep in their vineyard, that pastors would encourage their church to read and live out the concepts taught, and not just the soul-winners God places in every church. The three books are a great tool in the hands of connect groups as a study, new converts, and even people close to salvation. Within its pages there are insightful ways to work with people from all stages of life with varying experiences, and therefore it's helpful for all leaders, including business people.

I know countries, political situations, personalities, histories and fellowship backgrounds, callings and giftings will all be different and to agree on everything is very naïve. So I encourage you to focus on what works for you, what helps you. Above all, be open to God, He will show you what you can best take away.

Finally, let me explain the three books. *Be the One* is an entrée. It activates the tastebuds. It starts with an overview of testimonies and its spread is diverse and delectable. The reason for this is I want to show you how to work with a wide range of people because people are so different and we need to be appropriate when dealing with them. In regard to the tools, we cover a number of big concepts that really only scratch the surface. It's like the beginnings of a sculpture: we get the arms and legs, but not the big picture or the intricacies; that comes in the other two books. My personal salvation story is also in this first book and while I never wanted it to be the focus in the body of work, in this entrée it has become a feature, because without my story you cannot understand why soul winning is so important to me. Like any good explanation, it brings context.

Book two, *Who Wins The One*, is the main meal; this is where we deal with the big stuff, the *whys* and *hows* of soul winning. Book three, *For The One*, is the dessert and cheeseboard, providing more fantastic stories where we dig into deeper truths and do the fine tuning, bringing it all into a satisfying conclusion.

These books are beneficial for any time frame but I believe extremely more so for today. There is unprecedented darkness coming over the world and only a genuine application of these teachings by believers will impact the thousands of people who are without Christ in these foreboding days.

Deep down, genuine Christians really desire to win their friends, family and workmates to Christ. Unfortunately, most believers struggle with intimidation, fear of rejection, unbelief, and not knowing what to say or how to say it. Yet when they do see a friend or family member won to Christ it becomes a highlight of their life.

I was having dinner not long ago with a man who has done extraordinary things with his life, but one of the greatest highlights was seeing his closest friend become a Christian. It took 18 years and now his friend has won his family and they are all going on in Christ. As he told me the story he was radiant with such joy it lit the room up. It was a pinnacle moment in his life. That experience is one of the reasons why I've written this book. I want every believer to experience this type of joy—not once, but often. The joy of heaven, as they celebrate a soul won.

Be The One is a legacy of things learnt over a lifetime. I now hand it down to all who have ears to hear.

Enjoy the adventure and *be the one*,

Andrew

PART
ONE

THE ICE MAN

I MET THE ICE MAN on the island of Saipan. It was hard to miss him. A very tall man built like a bodybuilder. The locals came up to his chest and they were brown, so he really did stand out but especially because he was the only other white person I'd seen on the whole island.

It was my second trip to Saipan, a beautiful island, close to Guam and part of the Marianas group of islands. It's famous for a beautiful swimming grotto but far more famous for being a major battleground in the Pacific conflict in World War II. There's a very moving memorial honouring the fallen soldiers with the words to the effect of: 'Better to light one candle than curse the darkness.' That week I was speaking at a rally bringing the light of the gospel into the darkness.

I passed the Ice Man in the Galleria Duty Shopping Centre, a place where the rich and famous shopped and I simply looked with longing. He was obviously shopping, wearing the best and latest of the most expensive labels and looked very handsome. He was like an advertisement for Ralph Lauren. I couldn't help myself and in a moment of jest I said, 'Greetings, fellow white man.' We both laughed and began to chat and soon decided to have a coffee.

He was originally from the UK but was now based mostly in Southeast Asia. He had mainly worked in the British army and the UN peacekeeping forces and done many tours of duty. He was also a very wealthy man and delighted in showing me pictures of his many trophies, houses, boats, jet skis and Harley Davidsons. In a burst of creative witnessing I decided to show him pictures of my trophies, pictures being the stories of people who were now believers in my then-current church. They included criminals, bikies, a world champion kickboxer, bouncers and even world class engineers to name a few. They were amazing trophies, bad backgrounds but now doing great things for God and in the church, winning and serving people in the community and beyond.

The Ice Man went quiet for a while. Then after winning some sort of an inner battle, he decided to open up about his life. Ice Man was in Saipan to smuggle two high quality Thai cooks into Japan for a friend who operated a restaurant in Tokyo. His real story began when he joined the British Army as a young man. He had come from a poor family and had risen up the ranks. He was posted to Ireland nearly a dozen times in the midst of the 'Troubles.' In his first posting his best friend had been captured by the IRA and badly tortured. His head was delivered to the barracks in a box with his private parts in his mouth. Special forces ended up tracking down the perpetrators, he was witness to the devastating paybacks.

The things Ice Man saw and shared with me were so bad they kept me sleepless for several nights. They were dangerous and harrowing times and his many tours to Northern Ireland created significant tension and terror. He was later shipped out to the conflict in Bosnia working with the United Nations, yet again exposed to unspeakable tortures and cruelty in the 'ethnic cleansing.' This time it was not just soldiers but civilians, even children, and the UN were 'protectors' in word only. Again I was kept awake by the torture and injustice he shared.

It was now about 3pm in the afternoon, and, as a guest preacher I always go to my room to pray and prepare for the evening meeting. However, due to the obvious 'divine' interruption or appointment I put my preparation on hold and trusted God to give me extra grace for the meeting, since Ice Man was really opening his heart, it was important to follow through.

He shared that, without the help of a handful of sleeping pills, these horrors kept him awake for nights at a time. In fact most nights were spent with a gun in his mouth, praying for strength to end his life. What kept stopping him was a film featuring Robin Williams called What Dreams May Come. It dealt with life after death and in particular, hell. He didn't want to risk going to hell by taking his own life. I asked him if he spoke to any other friends that had experienced the same events. He replied 'no'— all of them had committed suicide. They'd been unable to deal with all they'd experienced. He was the last one alive.

At present, Ice Man was living in Southeast Asia, the head of a powerful drug ring, dealing pleasure drugs to the rich and famous. He had a greatly privileged life, numerous beautiful women, huge connections and a very clever network and operation. He was called the Ice Man for his cool nerve and disregard for life.

In talking to the Ice Man, I was aware of an extra dimension of grace. My words had divine life, attraction and insight, beyond what I normally sense when dealing with such witnessing situations. I was puzzled by this extra anointing. Finally it dawned on me and I asked him if anyone was praying for him. He responded immediately, his sister had breast cancer two years previously, and became a Born Again Christian. She had been completely healed, and was praying non-stop for her brother since that day. This explained what I was experiencing. It was the power of her heartfelt prayers for her lost brother.

As Ice Man shared this information with me, God cut in and gave me a picture or vision in my heart. I saw God looking down on the world, like a large desk globe. He says, 'Who can I get to intersect, who will be an answer to his sister's prayers?' Suddenly God sees something and then leans in and exclaims, 'Yes,' and says, 'Andrew Purchase is going to Saipan.'

It nearly brought me to tears. What was amazing to me is that God knew if I met him, I would talk to him, and if I talked to him, I'd witness to him and if he was open, I'd implement the 'Baby on the Bin' concept and God could answer his sister's prayers.

This is trust. Now the basis of our salvation and our walk with God is our trusting Him. Sometimes the reverse is also true, it's about God trusting us with His people and purposes. Thankfully, I had been trustworthy and done what God had anticipated I would do.

By now, it was getting late and I really needed to get ready. I asked him if he'd like to come along and he accepted my invitation. It was an excellent meeting. The Ice Man sat at the back just trying to take it all in. It was very foreign to him. At the end of the meeting I went back to explain things to him, when a lady was brought to me with a horribly disfigured hand. I prayed with her and her hand completely unfolded and came back to normal in front of us. The Ice Man went from Mr Cool Cat to Mr Jaw Drop. He wanted Jesus so we sat down and I introduced them.

The next couple of days, I did the rest of the meetings, spent time with the pastor and his family and built as much as I could into the Ice Man without overdosing him. We exchanged addresses. He went off to Japan with his Thai cooks, and I went to Guam and Palau to finish my series of meetings. Both series of meetings went very well. When I arrived back in Australia, the Ice Man had mailed me and sent a bunch of gifts. He was still very excited and hungry. I sent him a bunch of sermons and some key books to help him become established and to flourish. I invited him to a significant conference I was attending.

In a short period of time things began to take off, he saw nearly all his friends converted, bought them Bibles and they became 'fired up' for the things of God and he began conducting new believer's studies with the materials I sent him. All his friends and connections were amazed that the 'Ice Man' had unfrozen, he was alive, transformed and radiating. He grew and his study grew and grew so much that he wanted to buy a building and call it the 'Andrew Purchase Church' which I said was very complimentary but probably not a good idea.

He also phoned his sister and explained how he met me and what had happened, and that all of his friends were coming to Christ. He also gave her my phone number and she phoned me and thanked me for being the answer to her prayers.

It was all shaping up well, and I was looking forward to seeing him in a month at the conference, when all of a sudden he totally disappeared, completely fell off the radar. To be continued.

⬄ Takeaway ⬄

- The Ice Man's sister prayed, fervent effective prayer is always the platform.
- I was going about my daily business when a fun gesture opened a God door, be interactive with the people around you & be quick to respond to Holy Spirit prompting.

- God found a willing vessel to answer those prayers, being myself.
- The Ice Man because of his wealth, looks and physique looked very together but behind closed doors he was in great need. Big lesson to learn.
- Different strokes for different folks, I've never used 'showing my trophies off' before that day or since, but it was right for that day, it turned the whole conversation to God.
- Be flexible when you have to. I changed my schedule because I was on a God-appointment.
- He needed the time to be listened to and needed to be able to process what he was hearing because of deep strongholds of false beliefs, grief and trauma he had packed down into his life.
- He was a 'beachhead convert' as he opened the way for many others.
- The power of a miracle: the woman's deformed hand healed in front of him shifted things.
- Lastly and mostly importantly, he was followed up. The baby on the bin was in action.

Your Thoughts

Take a moment to ponder what you've discovered from reading this story. Is there someone in your community, like this, you could connect with or at least begin to pray for and see what Holy Spirit wants to do?

Tool
THE BABY ON THE BIN

Behold, a sower went out to sow ... fell on good ground and yielded a crop: some a hundredfold, some sixty, some thirty.

Matthew 13:3,8 NKJV

IN THE TOOL BOX there are a wide range of different tools and different precepts I've learned from being at the coal face over the years. The first one I want to share with you came from a simple prayer as the pricelessness of my new found salvation began to dawn on me. I wanted to grow in God and make heaven my home and I also wanted others I loved to join with me.

Becoming a Christian was unexpected, I was living in a hospital, crippled in a wheelchair, filled with darkness and pride. I was trying to disprove the Bible to some of my friends who had become 'born-again' and were now shiny, happy and together. However in the process, truth and light broke through the darkness and lies. Now, I was 'born-again', experiencing a series of powerful revelations that helped shape me for the rest of my life.

I had been heavily involved in eastern mysticism and new age but as I understood the Scriptures I repented deeply and received Christ as Lord and Saviour. Hell had been escaped and heaven was now my home. God was my Father not my judge, and I was His prized and loved child. The gaping emptiness in my heart that drove me incessantly to seek more, was finally filled. He was continually meeting me and delivering me from the layers of strongholds that had ruined my life and bringing me into His freedom.

I wanted to share Christ but I noticed many of the people who gave their lives to Christ at church did not always return, even though there was a tremendous 'follow up' program in play. Thankfully some did and it was a powerful thing to see them transform and go on but, sadly, often many didn't.

I wanted my friends and family to be built on 'The Rock', not the sands Jesus speaks of at the end of Matthew 7, to be the wise and ready virgins and not foolish ones as in Matthew 25. I didn't want the seed I was sowing stolen, but to take root and not die from distraction, this being the battle of the first three soils of the parable of the sower in Matthew 13. I wanted to witness and win them and, if at all possible, go on to become the 30, 60 or 100 fold.

I began to pray and ask Him to help me. A month later God answered those prayers. I had shared the Gospel with a man quite new to town. He was in his twenties, a thinker and quite responsive to the things of God and we chatted at length. As we said our goodbyes and I began to walk away the Holy Spirit quickened an intense picture to my mind:

I was in an alleyway between two old rundown buildings with graffiti covered walls, trash cans and dumpsters overflowing with rubbish and rats hunting for food. On one of the trash cans was a baby, vulnerable and beautifully dressed in clean baby clothes. It was in stark contrast to its surroundings. As I wondered where the baby's mother was, the Holy Spirit spoke to me and said, 'Would you leave a baby on top of a rubbish bin if you found it?'

It took a few seconds but then I grasped what He was saying: 'You wouldn't leave a vulnerable baby there but bring it to a safe place' likewise 'don't leave or walk away from an open, vulnerable sinner who you've placed the living words of God into.' It was about following up the 'open' people I met, so I raced after him and asked for his details and followed him up.

At this revelation I made a serious and lifelong commitment to God. It changed my life and those of many other people: I promised to follow up on any non-Christian who showed interest in the things of God as best I could. From that moment it was like God said, 'Here's someone I can entrust my precious lost sheep to' and an amazing fruitful journey began.

Every situation or person was different so wisdom was needed for traction to be achieved. Sometimes it meant going back to their shop or catching up outside work. Other times it meant keeping an eye out for them at the gym or if the connection was good and the interest was high I'd get a phone number and make room for a coffee or a visit. Essentially I did whatever was best and wisest for that person, but the key was making sure I followed them up.

I know this sounds basic, but so few people follow up.

This is not just a key for soul-winning but so many other things in our lives. It is important to follow up on what God is saying to us. That's what stops us from going round and round the mountain. Disciples grow according to their openness, hunger and ability to follow through on what they've been taught. It's also a foundational block to a successful marriage, family, business and a host of other things.

> 'In business, you'll be ahead of the rest if you attend to the simplest of things like responding to an email or text; very few people manage to do this and yet it makes all the difference.'
>
> —*Beau Wetter*
> *(Successful business owner and friend)*

I found this to be true when working for a season in commercial real estate. When I surveyed what potential clients most wanted, they responded with, 'Follow up.' I made this my goal, word got out, and I became sought-after. Often the doors to the future will open when you're faithful to follow through what's in front of you.

In the process of following up with open people, I'm able to discern or understand their level of interest and the situation they're in. From here, I am able to tailor the things of God to them and work with them in such a way they not only understand but desire more of the things of God. I am able to answer concerns, and help with misinformation and false beliefs that hinder them from moving forward.

None of this would happen if they weren't followed up. Following up someone gives you the connection and capacity to take it to the next level. It's not just witnessing it's also about developing a genuine connection of care and interest. People trust you when they know you care about them.

This trust allows me to know when they are ready to make a strong and informed commitment to Christ; that it's not just emotional but well thought out and for the duration. God faithfully meets with them powerfully and uniquely.

The good news is they grow in God, join church and excitedly take the things God is doing in their lives to all their family, friends and workmates bringing them to Christ and church like moths to a flame.

This takes place because of follow up. Remember the context here, these are people who are your regular points of contact and can be followed up—that is, you have the time and access to build the relationship. It's the people at work, the waitress where you buy coffee or people at the gym and a host of other connection points.

Heavenly Father, help me to love the lost like You do. I ask for joy and the boldness to communicate to those around me. I ask for the ability and burden to follow up those divine appointments Your eye is upon. I also ask for wisdom in working with each person's degree of openness and appetite and feed them appropriately. Thank You for answering this prayer and for making me a fruitful and effective believer.

In Jesus' name,

Amen

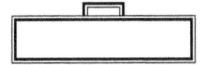

Story
THE ICE MAN, CONTINUED

SUDDENLY THE ICE MAN had vanished and I had no connection to the people he knew in Thailand. I had no way of contacting him and his sister didn't either. We both kept praying and entrusting him to God. Around six months later I received the most amazing letter from him. In fact it was an amazing two letters in one.

First he had written me a letter but for some reason had addressed it to a church in Perth, Western Australia. I was living in Brisbane at the time on the other side of the country. He had addressed it to a church I've never had any dealings with, however the secretary of the Church just happened to have been a flatmate of my sister some twenty years earlier.

I had come down to Perth from Geraldton, to stay a couple of days with my sister and while I had a good time catching up with my sister, her flat mate and friend was intrigued about how I'd become a believer, this led to many deep conversations. She was smart, argumentative in a good way, and funny. Throughout the couple of days I was there I worked through a number of issues that hindered her, and built a decent case for Christ. It wasn't enough for her salvation at that time, but enough to have a good impact. I went back home to Geraldton and my sister not long after started a job in London.

My sister's friend explained in her letter that while she lost contact with my sister, the things I shared with her had deeply impacted her and stayed with her. She had wrestled with them for a couple of years, during which time she struggled to party and 'get high' successfully. Eventually she went out and bought a Bible, prayerfully read it and soon came to meet Jesus. She started to go to a local church, in time met and married a good man who later became a pastor, and she was now the church secretary loving the Christian life.

She had always wanted to let me know what had happened in her life, and how she was now fully serving God but had no idea where either I or my sister was. When the letter arrived addressed to Andrew Purchase she decided to track me down. She soon found an Andrew Purchase in Brisbane, pastoring a church and sent her letter explaining her conversion along with The Ice Man's letter to me. I was extremely happy and touched by her letter but in awe of the incredible 'coincidence.' If it had gone to any number of other churches I'd have never received The Ice Man's letter or heard her story.

It was so nice to know that a seed sown so long ago was now bearing good fruit.

Equally I was just as amazed by the Ice Man's letter. Since being converted he was a transformed man. He won his friends to Christ and was radically changed. He had stopped bribing judges and police, and wouldn't deal in pleasure drugs anymore. He 'wanted out' of the whole business and the crime organisation he worked for said he could go as long as he did one final job for them. He agreed, and was sent quickly to Belgium. The 'final job' was essentially payback for the disruption his salvation and fruitfulness had done to the lucrative drug trade he'd been in charge of. It was a set-up to get him out of the picture all together. This set-up resulted in him being arrested and the Ice Man was now sitting in a maximum security Belgium jail with a hefty sentence. He had written to me from his Belgium jail cell.

He explained the situation to me in the letter, and also asked me if I could send him some more sermons to listen to whilst seeing out his sentence. I sent back a bunch of church meeting messages I and other speakers had preached. He wrote back in a little while, asking could I please send more as many of the other prisoners were listening too and they all wanted more. I sent a bunch more along with other quality material to read.

He responded again saying that people all over the jail were now getting saved and were listening to the messages and growing. The same thing that had happened in Southeast Asia was now happening in Belgium. He was what I call 'a beachhead convert' and revival had broken out in the Belgium jail. Despite the set-up and finding himself in a maximum security jail he kept his faith, had grown, and at the same time taken many others along with him.

The Ice Man was a walking altar call and an establisher of souls for the kingdom.

⬡ Takeaway ⬡

- Over the couple of days with my sister's friend I was able to work false beliefs and plant some decent seed in her heart. God watches over His Word, and the word sown deep bears fruit.
- While I was limited in time I helped build in the Ice Man the capacity to continue in the midst of great reversals and injustices.
- Following up after salvation is equally important. I discipled him from a distance with books and messages and letters from myself and other pastors.
- He was a genuine beachhead in both places and both places were difficult.
- When you can't follow up the power of prayer and entrusting people to God is paramount.

☁ Your Thoughts ☁

What have you discovered? How can you apply these takeaways to your harvest field?

> Tool

MEETING YOUR FUTURE SPOUSE and STRIKING GOLD

*And when Jesus came to the place,
He looked up and saw him, and said to him,
"Zacchaeus, make haste and come down,
for today I must stay at your house."*

Luke 19:5 NKJV

WHAT CONSTITUTES A 'baby on the bin'-type person? In one sense it's quite simply an interested person, but like everything else it's easy in theory so let me unpack it in a couple of illustrations.

One good illustration is when one meets their future spouse. Largely, it's never a big or elaborate plan, but an unexpected connection, an attraction or a conversation that's different, leaving each person with a song in their heart. You both come away saying, 'I enjoyed that and I want to spend more time with them.' Some people know from the moment they meet they will marry. However, most people need a few more dates and conversations.

Similarly, sometimes a person who's open will react quickly. They want to know Jesus and be part of His Kingdom and mission. Yet other times it's in the process of a few conversations that they get some traction. What's important is that both recognise something has transpired in the meetings.

They see or feel the truth or God's light, maybe His drawing or a feeding to their soul, a touch of freedom and hope. It could be any number of things that connect them to God. They will also go away intrigued, pondering what they've seen and heard and, if the connection is significant enough, will tell their spouse or close friend. That's a good sign.

This tells me I've stumbled onto a potential 'baby on the bin' person, a lost sheep in the midst of the goats, and like meeting your future spouse there's a desire to catch up again. So I follow them up.

In a sense it's a little like the healing of the woman with the issue of blood in Mark 5. Jesus sensed virtue had left him and she knew she was healed. There was a transfer or residue of God's virtue and they both felt it.

In the story of Zacchaeus Jesus recognises his interest for he has sought a better vantage point to see Jesus. His interest has lifted him above the crowd and made him visible. This is a wonderful picture of what I'm talking about. Zacchaeus is a 'baby on the bin' and Jesus' response is to follow him up and go to his house. Jesus touches his heart, and immediately he begins to testify of his changed life to his friends.

It's different with each person—sometimes it's

big and other times it's small. However, you begin to recognise it, especially as you get more experienced. You'll see this process play out in the stories. It was obvious, like the Angry Biker (whole story appears in book two) who told me he and his wife wanted to know about the Book of Revelation and could I come and help them understand. The Dux of the school was more abstract. She wanted to know the meaning of life; it popped up in the conversation we were having when I ordered coffee and it was enough for me to keep going back and work it through with her.

Another practical illustration is when the fishing line goes taut or jumps when a fish bites on the end of your line. Sometimes it's a small nibble and other times it's a big bite, so you react accordingly. I come to attention, step back and yield it to God and zero in on that subject and see where that leads.

It's similar with a metal detector. I've got a small Gospel-detector always humming away in the background of my heart. As I connect with people in my day sharing life and conversations, then if there's a 'beep' in my heart from the detector I know I need to zero in on what's just happened.

It all begins with learning to connect with people and sharing your life and being interested in them and while this is getting increasingly hard due to mobile phones and the social climate, you can still connect with people and find the open doors.

By the way I often wrestle with the fear of rejection. Certain things in my upbringing do not help—but we can't live in excuses or be victims. God grows, heals and changes us so we can fulfil His purposes on earth. Christianity is about transformation and serving people. I had to grow. I had to confront my weaknesses and change. This is always a humbling experience but a rewarding one too.

The bottom line is: get out of your comfort zone and learn to talk to the people around you in your life, listen for the divine connection and God's appointment and follow them up.

> *Heavenly Father, help me be alert and alive to open people around me who are alive to You. Help me to sense the jump of the fishing line or the beep of the gold detector when a person is interested. Help them to see and hear Jesus in me and help me to see their needs and interest. Help me not to miss or pass by lost sheep who are wanting to be found.*
>
> *In Jesus' Name,*
>
> *Amen*

Story

THE PSYCHIATRIST

SEVERAL YEARS BEFORE I MET the 'Ice Man' I was invited to preach through-out the north-east of America, then Phoenix, L.A. and finally San Diego. On my way to Rochester I had a very long layover in LAX Airport. I decided it was enough time to get lost and found, so I checked my baggage only taking my briefcase. I caught a bus and soon was passing names and sights I'd seen only in movies. We soon stopped at the famous Santa Monica Pier and I decided to get off and have a look. I walked down the pier and people were literally running to get out of my way. It took me some time to figure they were all in summer attire and I was totally in black. I'd come from a cold Melbourne winter wearing a long black coat, black boots, black shirt and black sunnies and carrying a black briefcase. I looked like a mafia assassin on his way to a 'job'.

I bought a coffee at the coffee shop at the end of the pier and noticed the couple next to me. She was wearing the same cap I'd just bought and he had the same T-shirt I owned. We said 'hi' and chatted about caps and T-shirts and we shared our lives and why we were in LA. They were from Phoenix, Arizona, and were in L.A for a conference. He was a psychiatrist specialising in multiple personalities, in particular the criminally insane. The conference went for three days and he'd scheduled a day's break at the end, had flown in his girlfriend, hired a convertible for the day and was now drinking coffee with her on the pier. They were dropping the car off at the airport that evening at the same time I needed to be at the airport and invited me to accompany them sightseeing for the rest of the day. How could I refuse? So I had an amazing day seeing the best of Los Angles in a convertible with some great people, having great conversations and then dropped back to the airport, on time with plans to catch up in Phoenix. It was an amazing God set-up.

I spent two weeks in the Northeast doing the meetings. They went very well, with lots of breakthroughs. One noteworthy thing happened. Right in the middle of preaching, the Holy Spirit interrupted me, and said the sound guy was going to kill himself that night and I needed to pray for him. For a couple of minutes, I had this major battle going on within but three times I heard the still small voice of God say the same thing so I stopped preaching and asked him to stand and explained what the Holy Spirit said to me. There was a hush across the crowd and then he began to weep and say it was completely true and had even purchased the rope that day to hang himself that night. He came down the front and we prayed and he was set free.

I then flew to Phoenix and once established I contacted my new friend from the Santa Monica pier and set up a meeting time. He was looking worse for wear and told me his girlfriend had left him and he was broken-hearted. We cruised around Scottsdale, a suburb of Phoenix on his Harley before having some deep and meaningful conversations over lunch about relationships and the meaning of life. We met again the next day where I was also able to explain Bible perspectives about many things including multiple personalities which he quickly grasped. By this stage God was all over him and was really impacting his thinking. I asked him to come to the meetings and he said he'd try and get there. I left to prepare for the night.

I was speaking to around 600 people. In this church the pastor and the visiting speaker sat up on the platform. Just as we were starting the service, I saw my friend come into the building and talk to the ushers, they then escorted him down to the front row. He had dug out a suit from the 1970's. It was purple corduroy with huge lapels and was quite a sight with his long hair and beard. He was amazed at the size of the audience and, as he sat down, he saw me on the platform. I gave him the thumbs up which he returned and gestured to the large crowd in amazement and he gestured back. 'I can't believe you're speaking in front of all these people, dude.'

We all sang, I preached and then gave an invitation for people to receive Christ. Who came down to the front with his head bowed praying, but my friend, the Psychiatrist.

I prayed with him personally. He was profoundly touched and so was I. To be able to see the whole process beginning from a chance meeting in L.A to visiting his hometown Phoenix where I 'just happened' to be preaching and to be able to spend time developing his understanding, 'building the baby' so to speak and to also help him through hurt, all culminating in seeing him coming powerfully to Christ was a wonderful thing. Above all I was able to leave him in good hands.

◇ Takeaway ◇

- Begin with taking a risk. Leaving the airport: risk. Talking to people you don't know: risk. Cruising around L.A with people I've just met: risk. All risks, but no risk, no reward.
- Following up and building a good connection also created a platform.
- Never judge a book by its cover. He was eminent in his field, flush with funds and very cool, yet things changed. His girlfriend leaving him broke his heart, making him far more open and I was able to get on the same level with him and connect.
- Be bold and invite people. After laying as much ground work as possible, I invited him and the Ice Man to the meetings. Both came and both got saved.

Your Thoughts

Have you ever judged a book by its cover? Is there someone in your harvest field you think would never be open to Jesus?

THE SEED MUST GO IN

For with the heart one believes...
Romans 10:10 NKJV

I'VE ALSO DISCOVERED THAT to be most effective the seed of the Gospel must go into the heart of an open person. Sounds simple, but it's important.

A good illustration of this is in gardening, the soil must be dug up, the seed placed in the hole, covered and then watered. The depth protects it from birds stealing it, from the wind blowing it away and enables the roots to grow down, securing the plant and feeding it. As it continues to get water and nutrients it grows roots downward and its shoots upward. Its capacity to grow into full bloom is far more possible. Again, this is the whole concept of the parable of the sower in Matthew 13. All these things allow the seed to fulfil its destiny.

Similarly, when working with open people, the seed of the Gospel must be deposited into their heart, protected and grown. This requires Christians to come out from the comfort and security of their homes and churches and get their hands dirty in the rich fertile soil of interested people's hearts. This is actually a joy.

This is what Jesus did, He left the comfort and security of heaven and planted Himself and His words into people's lives, houses and hearts. He connected with them at a heart level and thus bore fruit. The Pharisees and religious leaders of Jesus's time did not receive Him or His words [John 1] especially at a heart level, which is why Jesus chose and worked with the disciples who did.

In Luke 9:44, Jesus tells them His words need to sink down into their ears. Meaning, His words needed to go into their heart for understanding, where they would have the capacity to change, as opposed to just giving mental assent to them or simply paying lip service. Understanding this principle, you'll not scatter the seed but more sow the seed and thus create a better harvest.

While banners, invitations, flyers, church signs, outreach and the like are a start and better than nothing, what is really required is something of a more connective nature at a heart level. To do that believers have to be more engaged with their communities, connect with the people of their world, their coffee shops, gyms and the like. Pay an interest in people, ask questions, listen and talk with them—basically love them. Without doing this, the word (seed) will not get to them, let alone at a heart level.

It should not shock us that this is the same dynamic at work in a baby's conception. The seed of the man doesn't work unless its place within the womb of the woman. I know it's simple but it's profound. It's only when the life-giving seed from the man finds the fertile egg within the woman that an amazing process takes place. A zygote is formed. It's the beginning of life and similarly it's like the life-giving word of God placed into the heart of a fertile and open sinner's heart—a process just as amazing. It's the beginning of the journey that leads to a spiritual new birth.

I've learnt and worked at connecting with all sorts of people to see this achieved and if there's traction, they want to talk, unpack stuff, make a comment, even argue in a good way. I listen carefully and begin to sow the seeds of divine life into their hearts in a way they'll best understand. Don't think this is always done with precision and slickness. Many times I'm scrambling as I'm trying to catch up with what has just happened, but it's better than a robotic disconnected programme, and the Holy Spirit is always faithful. He helps and He is extremely happy a believer is imparting life into the heart of His lost sheep.

If there's no interest, I don't let it affect me, I am still friendly and perhaps will try later. You don't need to have all the answers, in fact you never will have all the answers but what's important is to love people and know Jesus, to have some courage and wisdom and step into interested people's lives.

This is explained in Romans 10:10,14 NKJV—

For with the heart one believes unto righteousness, and with the mouth confession is made unto salvation...

How then shall they call on Him in whom they have not believed? And how shall they believe in Him of whom they have not heard? And how shall they hear without a preacher?

See the importance of the heart believing and also the need of the messenger to bring the message or see that heart? We all need to be messengers to those around us who have fertile hearts. Which is the theme of this tool and the book.

You'll see this happen over and over again in the stories, it is about finding the open people, the lost sheep and then sowing into their hearts. When they start getting it and growing, it's not hard or scary but very exciting.

Heavenly Father, help me to be aware of the open people around me and to sow the word into their hearts. Help me to be sensitive to You and others at a deeper level, to listen to both the Holy Spirit and those who are open. I trust you for the enablement and insight for each person.

In Jesus' name,

Amen

Story

THE FERAL SURFERS

BEFORE I BECAME A CHRISTIAN I was hospitalised with a disease called Reiter's Syndrome. I had been paralysed from my waist down including my right arm. A couple of months after I became a believer whilst in the hospital, I was healed after reading the miracles of Jesus.

To increase my strength and fitness from all the muscle wastage from being so long in the wheelchair, I decided to start swimming in the ocean every day. One day on the way there I noticed a large group of travelling surfers camping oceanside under the 'no camping' sign. Just as I was driving past them God spoke to me and said He wanted me to turn aside and witness to them.

So I turned my motorbike around and drove down to speak with them. As I drew closer my heart absolutely sank. These were a group of people who completely intimidated me. They were older than me by a decade and were wild feral untamed surfers. They had come from a place four hundred kilometres north called 'The Bluff'. It was a huge and very dangerous surf break on the edge of the desert. They lived in the caves and surfed the giant swells of winter. They lived on the local seafood and partied hard, taking all types of drugs and drinking themselves into heavy stupors. They feared nothing and no-one. They were the 'Hells Angels' of the surfing world. Suddenly I felt very small.

Everyone has someone or some group of people that intimidate them and these were mine. Even worse there wasn't just one or two of them but a small tribe. They were laughing, partying and brawling and all stopped and watched me as I pulled up on my ridiculous little 125cc motorbike. Inside me an internal storm was breaking out. I felt I was in a tiny boat and the wind was howling and the waves were pounding and I was about to capsize. As I walked towards them many thoughts were running through my mind and I very nearly turned around and rode off several times. How was I going to do this? Who was I going to talk to? There were so many of them! I was good at one-on-one, not a small tribe. But in the midst of the storm I chose to follow through on what God had said. Little did I know I was moving from an internal storm to an external storm.

As I parked and walked over to them, everyone had stopped what they were doing and were now intently watching my every move. I felt the size of David in Goliath's shadow. With a racing heart I stopped in front of them and, not knowing what to do next, I simply spoke out and began to share my testimony, Christ and salvation. Everyone was very quiet for about a minute or so. For a moment I was lulled into a false sense of security and then twenty or so feral surfers fearing nothing opened up on me firing two fully loaded barrels. Veins popping out of necks and foreheads. Screaming and shaking their fists at me, their beer spilling everywhere and swearing at me in such a way that would make sailors turn in their grave. The internal storm became an external storm and was threatening to overwhelm and sink me. But having won the internal storm I was more fortified.

Suddenly in the midst of the screaming one voice became louder than them all. The guy sitting in a chair stood and was now roaring above them all shouting for them to 'shut up' and be quiet or he'd beat the 'crap' out of them. After the threats of bodily harm they quieted. He was obviously the leader and was quite feared so everyone backed down. He sat down and said, 'Ok, now go ahead I want to hear this.'

So I started to explain and for a while I had their attention but slowly the murmuring grew in the background until it was on again. The tribe was again roaring ferociously, challenging and threatening me. The leader had to stand up, scream and threaten them with a beating until everyone was quiet again. He then sat down in his chair and said, 'Ok, go ahead, I want to hear this.'

This cycle happened several times until I couldn't think of anything else to say. Once I finished he thanked me and everyone else abused me and I jumped back on my bike and drove home.

On the way home at the same place God had asked me to speak to them God spoke again but this time it was a question. He said, 'Why did I ask you to do that?'

I replied, 'You wanted to reach the main guy?'

'No,' He said, 'That wasn't for them, it was for you. I don't want you to be intimidated by anyone. I did this to set you free.'

I'm not sure what happened to all those guys but I'm sure about what happened to me. I got a whole lot freer. This was a huge breakthrough and was a key steppingstone in helping me grow into the person God wanted me to be. Do I still get intimated? Of course! I don't think you ever get fully free of it, but I do know you can walk through it and overcome it.

What's also significant is that this happened with no other believers around, it wasn't in a church service or connect group, it was just God, myself and the Feral Surfers. No one would have known if I'd simply ignored the small still voice, which is easy to do when you're intimidated.

However, it's developing our ear to the Shepherd and being sheep that obey that's the basis of our walk with God, so says John 10. This is to be developed both in the public and the private, both around believers and unbelievers. I've come to know that it's in these times of private obedience that we hone the voice of God and see Him move. This helps us to be able to step into public times like having to call out the sound guy who had bought the rope and was going to hang himself as well as many other intimidating situations I've dealt with in my life and ministry.

 Takeaway

- Build the habit of obedience. Learn to recognise God's voice and have the courage to obey it.
- Sometimes God is trying to teach us more than the people we are trying to help.
- Someone is always open. There's always a lost sheep amongst the goats. In the midst of his friends making a fool of me, the toughest guy stood up for me and the message.
- Discern and still the storm. When something good is about to happen, there will be demonic forces sent to derail you from getting to those places or people of favour.
- The storm at the end of Mark 4 seeks to stop the disciples from reaching the demoniac in the territory of the Gadarenes in Mark 5. His testimony saw many come to Christ. He was a major beachhead for the Kingdom

 Your Thoughts

What have you realised from this story? What are you intimidated by? And what can you do to go forward?

Tool
THE UMBILICAL CORD OF LIFE

*I have become all things to all men,
that I might by all means save some.*

1 Corinthians 9:22 NKJV

THE BEST WAY I CAN describe the art of following up a lost sheep is the illustration of an umbilical cord. The umbilical cord connects the baby and the mother. It's the conduit whereby the necessary building blocks for growth are given to the baby.

Similarly, the umbilical cord with open sinners is a cord of connection and relationship. Through this life-giving cord you're able to feed and develop the baby Christian foetus.

They must have an appetite. This varies from person to person and you need to recognise this and feed them appropriately. Don't let your fears underfeed someone who is really into it or, in your zeal, overfeed someone when they have limited appetite. You must pay attention. Christians can get so caught up in what they are saying that they miss what's happening in the other person. Pay attention, be wise and let love rule.

When I meet someone open to God, I find out what will help build our connection or friendship, (the umbilical cord) and at the same time I am working out what they know or don't know about God and church. Find out what sort of appetite they have for the things of God and the best way they learn and communicate, Paul describes this as being all things to all men, 1 Corinthians 9:22, getting on their 'wavelength' or simply finding a way to be understood by them.

This sometimes can happen in the initial conversation. However that's rare. It generally takes several meetings, but it all really depends on the person. To do this, I call back to the place of contact, or perhaps phone, text or invite them for a coffee or whatever is appropriate depending on their desire for connection or friendship. This is what I call forming the umbilical cord and from there I start to feed the growing baby.

Another point to consider is the umbilical cord removes waste products, and essentially this is what I'm also doing. I build and feed them with Scripture and Kingdom principles in a way they understand, working with what is primarily of interest to them. I also help free them from false beliefs and strongholds that hinder and stop them coming to Christ. But to do this effectively and at a heart level, I've got to have a cord.

You will see this working all the way through each story. At the moment, I'm working with two guys, one is a knowledgeable health professional and the other is a hippy musician. I've known both for a while and lately they have opened their hearts and shared their concerns with me. I have listened and talked with them at length and given them appropriate material for them to digest. One is very research-oriented and I'm giving him books to complement his interests, the other has realised his need for emotional intelligence, so I've given him a book on this topic. Later, I will follow them up and discuss these topics again.

What is important in the context of this tool is I also gave them a jar of my wife's homemade grapefruit marmalade, truly remarkable stuff. These are small gestures that build the umbilical cord of friendship and as I've gotten older I've enjoyed this nearly as much as witnessing. There really is something in being a blessing and seeing other people light up when someone thinks of them.

Another thing my wife and I do at Christmas and Easter is make homemade Christmas puddings or rocky road chocolate with personalised cards and give them to the businesses and people we know in town. All enjoy the gifts but mostly that someone thought of them.

This doesn't take a lot of effort. Yet it brings great joy and traction. By the way, I don't always use food. It's generally what's handy and appropriate but above all it's done in the spirit of benevolence, not manipulation.

These things create and keep the umbilical cord of connection and friendship. This is a conduit enabling the baby to keep growing until it becomes full term and there is a 'spiritual' birth—and that's generally a little chaotic just like in natural birth.

Above all: I'm listening and paying attention, leaning into and learning about the things that interest them and sharing what I've learnt. I am quite curious and enjoy learning about new things especially when it builds a better bridge with the person to help them understand and bring them to Christ

> *Lord, help me love people in a deeper way, help me to carry the heart of God as well as the message of God. Help me love people in their uniqueness. I receive a new generosity and insight with people, knit my heart with lost open people enabling Your words to have greater power and a deeper entrance. Keep me from offence and use my life.*
>
> *In Jesus' name,*
>
> *Amen*

> Tool

WHY IS THE BABY NINE MONTHS IN THE WOMB?

> *Thus says the Lord God to these bones:
> "Surely I will cause breath to enter into you,
> and you shall live. I will put sinews on you
> and bring flesh upon you, cover you with skin
> and put breath in you; and you shall live.
> Then you shall know that I am the Lord."*
>
> Ezekiel 37:5–6 NKJV

WHY NOT A MONTH? That would be certainly easier! The simple reason is, that's the amount of time necessary for the baby to be able to breathe, function and live outside the womb.

Sometimes babies are born too early and they are very vulnerable. There are specialised machines and even specialist doctors and nurses who are trained to help these premature babies develop and survive.

There is so much literature about conceiving and having a baby. Go to any book store or online you'll find large volumes of information. Yet, very little information on developing a lost sheep in Christian literature.

While a human baby will spend nine months in the womb, I find 'spirit babies' are developed in all sorts of different time frames. Some are ready for birth in an hour, a day, some a week, others take a month and others a year and occasionally some many years like Mr Slow Burn (full story in Book Three).

It all depends on how much they know, how willing they are to learn, what is lacking and application. Just as it takes nine months for a baby to develop for survival, it takes whatever amount of time is needed to birth a spiritual baby. Be patient.

The Ice Man didn't require lots of time. His sister had prayed solidly for two years for him. That had a profound effect and he had desperate needs. He also had a revelation of hell, that stopped him suiciding. He also knew that mansions, money, the latest fashions, beautiful women, yachts and power weren't the answer to his healing. I was dealing with a shorter time process than I'd have liked. He needed to grasp what 'real' Christianity is, if he was to survive in the situation he was returning to. The point being, not everyone needs a long time or a short time, they need their unique time, one that is right for them to survive.

The paradigm shift is not to immediately go for a quick decision but aim for longevity. You want them to make the distance. In these stories it isn't just an invitation to a decision, but a process of growth which resulted in the birth of strong 'born again' babies who could make it.

You will see in the story of Mr Protection (full story in book two) that he needed a month or two of growth while his wife was so open I could have prayed for her on my first visit. I didn't because it was important for him to catch up with her, when he was ready I took them both to church and they were saved 'together' and have gone on in Christ powerfully 'together.'

On the other hand, I took the Angry Biker's wife (also in book two) to church earlier than him. Her conversion and subsequent transformation was a catalyst that helped strengthen his desire for the same thing. This then also resulted in fruit amongst their friends which was like a mini revival.

Interestingly I worked with both those groups of people at the same time frame and had to work with them very differently because they were so very different.

Each person has a different time frame—important and unique to them. It's important you grow to be able to learn to do this, not only in soul-winning but in all the realms of working with people e.g discipleship and leadership training, because working with people requires tact and timing.

The Handsome Lonely Surfer (coming up) knew more than anyone. So I naturally but mistakenly thought he would be quick to come to Christ. But the world held such sway over him and it took me some time to adjust my sails and prayers appropriately.

In Ezekiel 37:1–15 God builds his vast army through a process of layers and when they are ready the breath of the life of God comes upon them and they live. This is a good picture of what I'm saying. There is a process of building by the Word and then comes the breath or 'born again' experience and they are ready to fight and function.

So I prophesied as He commanded me, and breath came into them, and they lived, and stood upon their feet, an exceedingly great army.

Ezekiel 37:10 NKJV

The point of this tool is to show you that just as a baby needs time in the womb to develop to be strong enough to make it in the world, so too do spiritual babies. The time is different to each person, that is a skill you'll grow in as you develop your relationship both with them and with God.

Obviously, this is done where it's possible, if you have the time and capacity because of your job, routine and relationship then do it. If you can't follow them up, e.g. you're working away or on holidays or on an outreach somewhere, you have to use the time you have to maximum effect.

Many people in church have grown up in Christian homes and have a knowledge of God, a history of church. Because of that they don't always grasp the enormity of the battle someone from an unchristian background has in breaking free from their old life and coming into a new lifestyle of Christ and church.

Their lifestyles and friendships are completely in the opposite direction. They know about getting drunk or stoned and they don't talk about the things of God, sermons and their favourite worship song. It's very different music and a very different conversation. It is mostly very dark.

So to actually break years of habits, a lifetime of appetites and friendships, is very hard and often greatly contested. In nearly every story you'll read in the book I've watched friends, families and work mates try hard to get them back, by reasoning or bullying them, often embarrassing them and especially tempting them.

The people in the stories rarely came from a church background or family. This is why I've learnt to take the time so that when these things happen they are somewhat prepared and developed. They've made a solid decision, they've processed things, thought things through, and talked it out with me. So when they decide to follow Christ they set their face like flint. They've got some roots down, done business with God. It's something they want and will fight for and something they will stand up against the flow of old habits and all the mockery their friends heap on them.

At this point their friends start to recognise something real has happened and they need to be taken seriously. This is where there's a shift and where the seeds begin to be planted in their friends and as we see from the stories, their friends in time come to Christ and there is a move of God as they apply to their friends what I had done with them.

But the key was building or developing the open person enough so that when it was time to decide they could weather the storms and develop roots and habits.

Lord, help me to grasp that the process of salvation is different for each person. I receive wisdom and love enabling me to walk and work with people so I can grow them appropriately. Help me not to get too far in front of people that need extra time and help me to keep up with people that are growing more quickly than others. I trust You. I break fear and anxiety over my life and walk in grace.

In Jesus' name,

Amen

Story

THE DUX OF THE SCHOOL

IT'S IMPORTANT NOT TO BE pigeon-holed or limited to working just with a certain type of person. You have to be able to discern who is open and work with them whoever they are or whatever their background. We have to be able to adjust our sails. This is what Jesus did and, with Him working through us, we should be able too. This is why this story is so good. The Dux is the very opposite of most of my stories.

I met the Dux just before she became the Dux. She was working at a coffee shop near our church. I was visiting the café for the first time for an appointment. While she took the order we started to chat. She was in her final year of school studying hard and getting the highest marks. She was going to be a doctor. She talked with real passion about her future and about 'doing good' in the world, then suddenly she sighed and out slipped, 'Sometimes it's all just so empty to me.'

This is when the fishing line jumps in your hands or the metal detector beeps declaring precious metal under foot. I decided this is where I was getting my morning coffee from now on. So each time she was rostered on I took time to speak with her, and we began to talk about life, 'the emptiness of life' and the fullness of God.

I was very aware of 'the emptiness of life' before coming to Christ. It felt like there was an almighty chasm in my heart that never could be filled. I tried to fill it. I put the sex, drugs and rock and roll in there and that didn't work. I went travelling, hitchhiking around Australia and New Zealand. I saw oceans, deserts and mountains but nothing touched the emptiness.

I entered a Hindu ashram and lived there for nine months, but didn't find it there either. I read about Buddhism, got into fitness, football and surfing. I tried being 'cool', then university, but nothing came close to filling the massive hole in my heart. I certainly didn't think it would be Christianity. I was a voracious reader of history and 'The Christian Religion' had such bad stains. It took some time for me to understand that 'real' Christianity was about Christ, His power, love and His true church not religion.

Over the next few weeks I explained to her that it wasn't things, people or pleasure or education or even helping people that filled the emptiness but Christ. It was about enthroning Him in our heart, having Him fill the void and letting life flow from that.

I have discovered a very practical step when the conversation turns to the emptiness of life. Several times in a coffee shop throughout the world I've often used a napkin to draw what this looks like and so I've named this the 'Napkin Diagram.' I showed her the diagram which helped her understand what she was going through and looking for. There's a chapter on this later.

Each time I ordered a coffee and chatted, I built the relationship of trust and watered the Gospel seed. I listened to her heart and answered her questions. She was part-Filipino and had family and Catholic strongholds. I slowly helped her understand those battlegrounds which can really take out people as they begin to take off. Best of all, she was excitingly getting who Jesus was and what He had done, and how He could fill the emptiness, and give her genuine and true meaning. She began to respond. Solid traction was occurring.

At the appropriate time I asked some of the Christian girls in the church to start having coffee there too, and soon she was coming to church to check it out. When she met Jesus she was filled to the brim and glowed like a lighthouse. Her sister, who was a party girl, completely gave her life to Christ too. Her parents were impacted for good as she grew in Christ. She started to sing in one of the bands in the concerts and grew in all she did, many people were touched by her life and ministry.

She became the Dux of the very impressive school she was attending. She went on to study in the medical field and later married one of our best guys. Several years passed before they became pastors and then went on to become missionaries overseas.

Takeaway

- You don't have to be a 'bad' sinner to need the Saviour. The Dux was one of the nicest people I've ever met, very smart and extremely kind. But as good as the Dux was, she still needed Jesus as Saviour and Lord.
- Learn to hear more than words. There was a cry of an unfulfilled life.
- If you find an interested person, change your coffee shop or whatever, go to where they are for that season. They are more important than your ritual.

Your Thoughts

What did you take away from The Dux? Is there a young person in your local cafe who might be open or looking for the answers to life?

Tool
LOVE AND RESPECT

'You are the light of the world. A city that is set on a hill cannot be hidden. Nor do they light a lamp and put it under a basket, but on a lampstand, and it gives light to all who are in the house. 16 Let your light so shine before men, that they may see your good works and glorify your Father in heaven.'
Matthew 5:14–16 NKJV

THIS MIGHT SOUND SIMPLE, but I'm surprised at how many Christians are so harsh in their judgments of non-Christians. You must treat people with love and respect to have an impact or a voice. Too many believers are not interested or, even worse, prejudiced. Most of these people don't have the Christian heritage or teachings you've been exposed to.

Very few people will listen if they don't respect you. Learn to be a servant. Be generous and thoughtful. Remember people's names and what's important to them. Don't be nosy or moralise too much. Have a sense of humour, especially about yourself. Be inspiring, be a light in the darkness. Use wisdom, share your life, don't be ashamed but don't be stupid. Learn to handle being mocked or persecuted with good grace. Take it on the chin, rejoice, sometimes it's a compliment and sometimes it's a test. Often the people who gave me a hard time about being a Christian in my jobs are the very ones who later came to me with open hearts when their lives fell apart.

Try not to use Christianese or verbosity like Praise the Lord, Thank You Jesus, Glory to God and Hallelujahs every conversation. Most people are repelled by this type of talk, purely because they don't understand it.

Learn how to communicate Bible truths in a language and a way they understand and enjoy. This not only helps them but also pushes you to develop your own communication abilities. I've read that John Wesley first preached his sermons to the servants and hired help before he took them to the pulpit each Sunday, just so he knew he could be understood.

Learn about other people's cultures. Find out what sports teams people follow and keep an eye out for upcoming events happening on the weekend. These things are simple yet practical relationship-builders.

Be interested in others and be interesting. Pay attention to people's likes and dislikes, ask questions and read up on their interests. Do not be manipulative, moody or judgmental. Don't look down your nose or speak down to people. Realise there is a natural dynamic in you that people will respond to—Christ the Hope of Glory. He makes us lighthouses and safe harbours for people. (Matthew 5:14–16)

Stretch and grow, expand your heart and influence. Jesus said the Kingdom of God is like a wineskin. The key thought behind this is that a wineskin must grow and expand with the fermenting wine. Likewise we must be a people who expand with His Spirit, heart and love for people.

These things will help connect and give you a platform to be heard, but remember the key factor is their openness and the degree of their hunger. This is what separates the lost sheep from the goats and shows what level or intensity you can work with people.

If someone's not interested, don't let rejection or disillusionment beat you, simply enjoy them as a person, they might be open later. Focus on finding people who are open and work with them. Someone, somewhere is always open.

Heavenly Father, help me act in a way that inspires people around me to know You and reach out for You in a substantial way. Give me credibility and insight when working with people that I might have influence for You in their lives. I ask You to help me be the salt and light. To not be afraid to let my light shine and to fall afresh in love with people and getting to know them.

In Jesus' name,

Amen

THE HANDSOME LONELY SURFER

AFTER BEING SAVED FOR six months, most of my friends had now become Christians. They were all growing strong roots downward and bearing good fruit upwards. It had shaken our small town. Some people were inspired, many were bewildered and some were upset.

Since my supply of non-Christian friends had dried up, I was in a quandary about what to do next. Slowly it dawned on me I would have to extend myself and learn to talk to people I didn't know. This opened up a lot of questions for me like 'How would I do this?' or 'Can I share such personal information to people I'm not close to?'

I was going to have to venture out of my comfort zone. I looked around at the possible people. The one who came to mind was the Handsome Lonely Surfer. I would see him often at our local bar—or 'pub' as we call it in Australia. He had a 'cool group' with some very pretty girls. He was a great surfer, a very good painter and a talented drummer, but he had a deep sadness in the midst of all the popularity, talent and looks. I felt he was depressed, lonely, maybe even aimless.

I understood this. Before becoming a Christian I would spend night's riding my motorbike to different pubs in our town looking for 'this friend' who I later realised was Christ. Once Christ came into my heart, I was cured from doing this. I was going to heaven and God had a plan for me. I was filled with supernatural light, the darkness had been banished and God had breathed significance and value into and upon me. I was doing something honourable and noble, not seedy like my old life had been.

So I summoned my courage and bought a packet of chocolate biscuits called 'Tim Tams', ventured over to his house and crossed the threshold to meet hopefully a new convert. I stood at his door for some time, with the packet of melting chocolate cookies/biscuits in my hot nervous hands trying to figure out what to say. I hadn't been invited so this was pretty rude. What do you say in those situations? I didn't know as I'd never done it before. For several minutes I nearly walked away but in the end summoning my courage I knocked.

He recognised me and said, 'Andrew.'

I said, 'Hi, I thought I'd pop over,' and handed him the Tim Tams.

He looked at the biscuits and his eyes lit up. 'Great, come in.' That began a great adventure and friendship.

Turns out he knew lots about God—more than all of us put together. He had been brought up a Baptist and, at that stage, I had no idea what that exactly meant. I did know it meant he knew lots of the stuff I'd taken six months to learn. Two things whirled around my brain as we talked. One was: 'Wow, this was easier than I had thought.' The other, which I should have paid more attention to was: 'If he knows all this stuff, why isn't he powering on for God already?'

It was my first meeting with the world of religious Christianity—knowledge without action.

I went with the first and left excitedly after a couple of hours thinking how easy this was: the gold had been detected and would soon be dug up and our church didn't have a drummer and how good was God!

Surprisingly he didn't become a Christian quickly. In fact, he was one of the hardest people to come to Christ that I've ever witnessed to, and it was one of the most frustrating times that I can remember. Yet it ended up teaching me one of the most important lessons I've ever learnt in regard to soul-winning and being an overcoming Christian.

Weeks turned into months and we seemed to do lots of talking without going anywhere. So I started to become more creative and even commissioned him to paint The New Jerusalem coming down to earth in Revelation 21, thinking once he saw that he'd get saved. Nope. I tried several other things but all to no avail. I was greatly discouraged, confused and stopped visiting. Soon he saw some mutual friends in the surf and asked where I was, and said he was missing our chats. So I went back, yet nothing changed. All talk and no action.

But something did happen. A good friend of the Handsome Lonely Surfer moved in and amazingly his friend was more open than him and got powerfully saved. The conversion of Popeye the Scandinavian Viking was truly a sight to behold, one of the most amazing I've seen. I thought slyly to myself when the Handsome Lonely Surfer sees this, he will give his life to Christ.

To my shock he didn't. Yet amazingly he knew so much about God and salvation. The love of the world had wrapped its all-consuming controlling tentacles around his heart and life and they were overpowering his desire for God and the things of God.

By now six months had passed and I had tried everything and anything I could to win the Handsome Lonely Surfer. I was exhausted and fell on my face before God and told Him as much. I gave up and I said to Him, 'I can't do this anymore. I give up.'

'Good,' was His reply. 'I've been waiting for the last six months for you to stop trying so hard and let Me help you.'

I repented, surrendered afresh and completely released him to God's hands. Three days later there was a knock on my door. It was the Handsome Lonely Surfer with tears streaming down his face. He explained what had happened. His girlfriend had unexpectedly left him. In addition his father had sadly passed away. His Dad, who was quite elderly, walked close to God and had been a genuine Christian. Both his girlfriend leaving and his dad's death had shattered and woken up my friend's need to get right with God. He had tears pouring down his face as he asked me to pray for him. I took him inside and we knelt down and prayed. He prayed very sincerely, repenting and fully surrendering his life to Christ. He meant it and went on powerfully.

He is still saved today. He has been a tremendous support in his church and helped many people. He has played in worship bands as well as in outreach bands. He's seen many, many hundreds of people come to Christ. He has used his painting skills to paint many signs and murals.

In one church I pastored, the back of the building had a very old large wall facing a major traffic intersection and the town centre. It was at least two storeys high and an eyesore. We flew him over and he transformed this ugly wall with a massive mural. The newspaper did a front-page article on it and the mural became a major landmark for the area.

He is also a prolific surf board shaper and on every board he writes: 'Refuse the mark' Rev 13. The Handsome Lonely Surfer becoming a Christian was a major setback for the devil and it was like a big rock dropping into the little pond of our town. The waves rippled out, folks were stunned and impacted by his decision. The Handsome Lonely Surfer had become a Christian and a full-on one too.

More amazingly for me was, what I tried to do with all my heart in six months, God did in three days. So from then on before I ventured into anything I stepped back and invited God to go first. This became one of the greatest lessons I've ever learnt as a believer, and I continue to walk this out in everything I do, both big and small.

Takeaway

- You overcome your fears by facing them with God. You just have to do it. I knocked on the door.
- By extending my area of influence to others I didn't know opened a massive door for me in soul-winning. No longer did I have to either know someone or wait to be invited. Now I could invite myself—take some Tim Tams, go and be fruitful.
- From the moment I surrendered it shifted the capacity to God, not me. He is far more able. From this lesson, I don't wait until the end to surrender. I begin with surrender.
- When occasionally I forget and am back to trying too hard, I would remember I hadn't stepped back and let God go first. And God moves.

Your Thoughts

Who are you in contact with in your vineyard that might be lonely or searching?

When was the last time you stepped back and asked God what He wanted to do in the life of someone you are trying to reach for Christ?

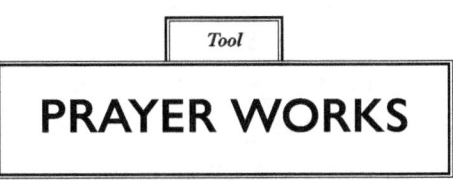

PRAYER WORKS

...the effective, fervent prayer of a righteous person avails much.

James 5:16 NKJV

I WILL LOOK AT PRAYER in more detail but let me lay a basic groundwork of the importance of prayer and its connection to God's power in drawing and directing, as in John 6:65 that no one comes to Jesus unless that person is drawn by the Father.

Often in the process of connecting with someone it becomes evident that the Holy Spirit is in the process of drawing and working with them and you've stepped into a divine appointment.

Sometimes this is because of the person's own prayers. There are many reasons why non-Christians pray, especially alone at night or in crisis. Sometimes they're seeking the meaning of life or needing divine help or asking God if He's real, sometimes they just need to unload their burdens. Please understand that God really tunes in and hears these types of prayers and

He loves to answer them and make Himself real to them and sometimes you are the answer to those prayers.

Sometimes this extra drawing power is because of other people's prayers. When someone gets converted they will begin to intercede for their friends and family and you might be the person God wants to use to answer their prayers, especially if you are living in the proximity of this person. Working with God in these situations brings an extra dimension of intimacy and grace which always makes the witness and working with them many times more remarkable. I saw this with The Ice Man, an extra overlay of anointing on my words giving them far greater weight. I later learnt this was due to his sister's prayers.

In reality every believer ought to be praying that God would be released in their world, drawing sinners to Himself and using and working through us to do great things.

Prayer above everything fills you with God's dynamic power as Jesus promised in Acts 1:8, enabling our 'oil lamps' to be full and our fires burning. There is something wonderful seeing the power and the fire of God emanating from someone. It's not hard to connect to the lost when you're filled with the Fruit of the Spirit: love, joy and peace. These are hard to contain and help me talk to the people in my world.

But if you're not prayed up, if you're empty, then there is little to give. I've found so much happens when I've taken the time to pray. I've got a cutting edge, a Holy Spirit spring in my step. I can overcome the fear of man which is a snare. It's a joy to share, not a burden.

Just as you need to be believing, yielding and working with the Holy Spirit, so too you need the authority of Jesus to shut down the devil and his minions. This is what Jesus was talking about when binding the strongman in Matthew 12:29, and when He spoke of binding and loosing in Matthew 16:19.

These demonic powers need to be bound and their influence marginalised so they can no longer steal, kill and destroy as described in John 10:10. They will try to steal the word and your open convert as in the Parable of the Sower recorded in Mark 4.

One of the main reasons Britain was able to win World War II was because they won 'The Battle of Britain'. They won the dominion in the sky above them. From there they pushed into European skies, this gave them dominion in the sky and on land. When you own the skies you're in a better position to overcome the enemy below.

Both you and the people you are praying for will have demonic skies or demonic forces at work to hinder, divert and nullify you. This is why prayer and, at key times, fasting is so important for both yourself and those you are called to win, build and birth.

All the stories are wonderful to read but let me tell you behind them is a solid base of prayer from the first meeting increasing as we come to the powerful conversion experience and beyond.

The stories and tools come from numbers of decades at the coal face. This book has been a decade-long process. Time has helped me unpack the tools with more clarity and has also helped me see the shifts in the world and church, that's why book two and three are so important. While the world certainly has been increasing in its darkness and demonic agenda, the prayer life of many believers and church has not grown in proportion.

Many of us are too easily sidetracked by Netflix and social media, sports and a host of other things. Most of these things are not evil but most have a huge capacity to distract us from individual and corporate prayer. These are the cornerstone of all Kingdom advances. Limited prayer, limited fruit.

The amazing story of The Cross and the Switchblade began with David Wilkerson being challenged by the Holy Spirit to switch off his TV and use the same amount of time to pray. Every season of revival in history through all ages is preceded with serious prayer, repentance and intercession.

I tell you, behind every one of these stories was a bank of prayer.

> *Heavenly Father, help me to pray effectively and fervently, help me to release the Kingdom of God in my life and in the lives of those I'm working with to great effect. Help me also to overcome the works of darkness, nullify their words and work. Help me to grasp the*

importance of prayer and pray accordingly. Help me to find others like-minded as there is great power in unity and agreement.

In Jesus' name,

Amen

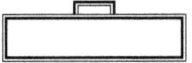

Story

POPEYE, THE SCANDINAVIAN VIKING

THE HANDSOME LONELY SURFER'S friend who moved in with him was from Scandinavia. He was like a Viking, very big and very strong. A shock of blonde hair and the biggest forearms I've ever seen. He was like Popeye the sailor man. His job was shovelling dirt all day, every day, so I assumed his massive forearms came from that. He never seemed to wear shoes, even in the middle of winter. He was also the local hash dealer in town. He moved in with the Lonely Handsome Surfer and soon became involved in our discussions. Amazingly he was more interested, so I continued to visit him more than the Handsome Lonely Surfer.

Around that same time, our pastor invited a man called Larry Reed from America to preach. He was called an evangelist, but we weren't sure what that meant. Still my pastor said he had a great story. He was an exciting 'out there' speaker and encouraged us to bring everyone we could, the wilder the better. He was true on both accounts.

Larry Reed was a big man, covered in tattoos before it was popular to ink. He wore the most colourful clothing we'd ever seen, bright yellow shirts and red pants with lime green socks! He had a big black moustache and a very deep, husky voice like he'd been smoking cigars and drinking whiskey all his life. He had been a heroin addict and sentenced to jail in the infamous San Quentin Prison. He told of his fear walking into the 'big yard' for the first time and hearing the hardened criminals yelling out threats and desires from their cells towering over the 'big yard'. It made our 'surfy boy' hair stand on end, and one thing was for certain, none of us wanted to see the inside of San Quentin prison—ever!

He preached in a rhythm like a machine gun, with all sorts of rhyming lines and we were all absolutely and completely enthralled. After Larry's salvation and release from jail, he bought a bus and built a preaching platform on top. On one side of the platform was written in massive letters 'THE BLOOD OF JESUS' and on the other side, 'JESUS LOVES YOU'.

He went around the cities of America, particularly the university campuses preaching and seeing hundreds come to Christ. He created a great move for God in the sex, drugs and rock'n'roll movement that was sweeping across the USA.

I invited both the Handsome Lonely Surfer and his new flatmate to the meetings but only Popeye the Viking came. He was enthralled and got saved that night. He was so touched that he leap-frogged barefoot over all the parking meters along the main street to home. The next night Larry Reed at the end of the preaching laid hands on him and prayed down heaven, he literally ran around in a circle on the spot with his hands lifted in the air speaking very loud in other tongues like in Acts 2. He was shining like a thousand suns. It truly was a sight to behold. That was when I slyly thought to myself that when the Handsome Lonely Surfer sees this, he will give His life to Christ.

He did not and I gave up, I let go and let God.

Amazingly, my new convert Popeye was immediately offered an incredibly high paying job. He was very excited about it, but it involved leaving town and going to the mines, a place where there was no church. In fact we began to see this happen regularly. Great job offers immediately after powerful salvations, always involving leaving town and going to remote mining sites with no fellowship. It took some time for our new converts to realise this wasn't an answer to prayer, but in fact the devil luring them away from what God was doing in their new-found Christian faith.

We also learnt it wasn't just jobs. Stunning girls wanted to jump into bed with our new male converts, and the handsome town Romeo was suddenly interested in newly saved plain Janes. The best drugs suddenly turned up in town and were made available to our newly saved drug-loving convert. Those with strong families, particularly Catholic, rose up to draw them away from their new-found faith. These were critical times and powerful temptations sent to steal the quality new converts. Fortunately nearly all of them overcame their temptation. I believe this was mainly due to the seeds sown pre-salvation because of the Baby on the Bin principle: following up and developing the seed.

Thankfully, Popeye rejected the offer and stayed, stopped dealing hash and grew in Christ.

⬡ Takeaway ⬡

- Sometimes you meet and win people in the process of witnessing to another.
- Be flexible and work with who responds.
- Be prayed up and pray for those you've won as the devil loves to steal away good converts.
- Make sure you've been sowing seeds into people so when a good speaker comes to your church you can invite a seeded person to hear the message.

☁ Your Thoughts ☁

What can you take away from this story? Are you prayed up ready to go out into your harvest field?

Tool

DON'T WASTE SIX MONTHS

*Behold, now is the accepted time;
behold, now is the day of salvation.*

2 Corinthian 6:2 NKJV

A LITTLE WISDOM I learned along the way was that many believers think that, if they just love on people, they will respond and become Christians. A friend in church in the early days decided to do this with a gentleman he worked with. They became great friends and did many things together. After six months he told the man he was a born-again Christian and shared the Gospel. His new best friend terminated the friendship.

Another true story illustrates this point. John, a believer, met Dan a non-believer, whilst doing his daily run. They talked, found they lived quite close and both loved running, so they began to run regularly together and it developed into a great friendship.

John wanted to talk about his faith but didn't. He kept putting it off and many months went by. Finally he could bear it no longer. He went around to share Jesus with his friend Dan and was surprised to see a large removal van taking furniture from his friend's house.

He went to ask what was going on. His friend replied his marriage had broken down and they were getting a divorce. John began to share his faith. Dan listened patiently for a while then lifted his hand and stopped John. 'Why didn't you share this six months ago when we first met? This had power to change me and save our marriage but you come now when it's too late.'

This doesn't mean I launch into my testimony or the plan of salvation every time I meet someone. Conversely to wait six months is not wise either. I try to be interested and interesting, and because I love being saved it flows from me somehow in the flow of conversation.

It's really important to grasp that what saves people is the Gospel. Yes, it is supplemented with service, love and helping people but, if you just love people and not share your testimony or the Gospel in some way, you are only doing half the job.

Thank God there are people doing good, it's great and that's more of a mercy ministry but if you're seeking to use it as a tool to witness, understand it needs to be complemented with the Gospel. You can see this play out in the story, The Late Night Fright (see book three).

The Gospel needs to be planted and unpacked, watered and guarded for it to bear fruit. Sometimes that goes across current cultural thinking but it's biblical and it's what causes people not only to be born again but grow. This is what both the church and the world need today.

Lord, help me to seize Gospel moments in life. I reject fear and timidity. I ask for wisdom, love and boldness. Help me not to be ashamed of Your words and help me to make Your word desirable to those whose hearts are seeking You. Help me overcome my fear of rejection and share what You have done in my life with interested people around me. Help me to know the right time to share.

In Jesus' name,

Amen

Story

MAD THOMMO AND THE SCARY BIKIE

MAD THOMMO

HE WAS CALLED MAD THOMMO because he was just that—mad. Although, you would never say that to his face, ever! He was the most feared man in town. Mad Thommo wasn't a tall man but he was extremely wide and very tough. Cancer had eaten out part of his back by the time he was in his late 20's and he was just an overall unusual character.

I distinctly remember the day I first laid eyes on Mad Thommo. A fight broke out in the tavern where I worked between Mad Thommo and a man who was about 6'6" and extremely well-built. It would appear that Mad Thommo was going to get beaten up. But suddenly Mad Thommo jumped up and grabbed the man in a headlock and with his sheer weight pulled him down. Then, he ran the big man headfirst into a brick wall, knocking him out. That was my first lesson in understanding why he was so feared.

One day when I was still a young believer and pre 'the baby on the bin' experience, God told me, 'I want you to go around to Mad Thommo's house and tell him about Me.'

Now I didn't know Mad Thommo enough to go to his house. I knew him only as a 'hello' passing by in the street with a quick retreat. After God said this to me, I had to battle waves of panic sweeping over me. I said, 'Lord, anyone but Mad Thommo.' But God was persistent and His still small voice stayed constant and clear, 'Go and see Mad Thommo.'

I lived in the holiday apartments near the lighthouse on the peninsula, and Mad Thommo lived nearby. On my way to his place I was trying to work up the courage to knock on his door. My palms were sweaty, and a migraine headache began to pound in my brain. I felt like I'd aged five years in twenty minutes. But I obeyed, very reluctantly.

Slowly and fearfully I walked around and knocked on Mad Thommo's door. My heart was beating, my mouth was dry and I had a raging headache. It felt like an eternity waiting for him to answer. Mad Thommo opened the door, recognised me and said: 'Andrew, come on in.' Once I was seated, he said, 'I've just cooked up some pumpkin soup and home baked bread, would you like some?'

I just about fell off my seat in shock! I thought Mad Thommo would have rather ripped the leg off a wild pig and eaten it raw, such was his notoriety. But no, he even baked bread. He ate homemade pumpkin soup.

Something I imagined doing at my grandma's house. I obviously didn't refuse his hospitality. We sat down and I began to eat the soup and bread, which was delicious. After watching me for some time Mad Thommo said, 'Well, Andrew, what's been happening in the church you've started going to?' He followed that comment with a wink, 'Any good-looking girls there?'

Again, I nearly fell off my chair in absolute amazement. Trying to not look too stunned, I ignored his last question and began to explain the different things that were going on in church and shared Jesus with him. He was all ears and appeared to drink in my stories of salvation and the things that were taking place.

Later Mad Thommo was hired at the Pipe Coating Factory where I was working and he saw a number of remarkable conversions and heard the Gospel on numerous days. Not long after that Mad Thommo passed away from his battle with cancer. I'd like to believe he is in heaven (God was certainly emphatic about me going and witnessing to him). He certainly heard the Gospel message and was surprisingly open.

The amazing thing for me was that while he was an extremely tough guy, he was also very open to God.

THE SCARY BIKIE

Another encounter highlighting the fact that 'people are never what they appear' occurred when I was living in Sydney. We were doing an outreach in Rockdale and talking with people on the street, all except this huge bikie. He was probably 6'6" a very big and strong man with scars on his face. He was lounging around on a big Harley with full leathers looking very dangerous. He was a scary dude. Everyone was giving him a wide berth. I hate that feeling of intimidation so to break it I eventually went over to talk to him. We chatted about bikes and stuff for a while and then we ended up having a heart-to-heart conversation where he shared his previous life.

He had worked in the banking industry in a very senior position. He often had to travel. Many times on returning home he would find his wife in bed with another man. Eventually, it created such angst he had a breakdown, lost his job and his life as he knew it. He got involved with drugs, alcohol and ended up in an outlaw bikie gang. So here I was sitting with this huge intimidating bikie who had been scaring the whole street. Tears were in his eyes as he shared his heart with me. I remember thinking how different this man really was compared to the rough and tough exterior he was portraying. I tell both these stories as they highlight what people appear to be are often different to who they are. Many of the greatest converts don't look like the person they truly are on the inside.

 Takeaway

- Develop a hearing ear and be obedient to the voice of God.
- He knows people's hearts better than we do.
- Don't judge a book, or person, by what they look like. Tough doesn't mean they're not open to God. If possible, find connection points that open deeper conversations.
- Fight intimidation. Be wise and not fearful, take the step of faith and God will give you the words and you might just find a lost sheep.

 Your Thoughts

What did you discover from these stories? How can you go deeper when chatting with the lost in your vineyard?

Tool

NOT INTERESTED IN CHURCH BUT OPEN TO JESUS

> *But when they saw it, they all complained, saying, 'He has gone to be a guest with a man who is a sinner.'*
> Luke 19:7 NKJV

YOU'LL SEE THIS IN quite a large number of the stories. People weren't initially interested in church. Yet in time as I worked with them this changed and not only did they come but brought many others too. This is important because for many believers asking someone to church is their main way of evangelism so when someone doesn't want to come they think they are not interested.

Yet, in talking with them I found an openness. The 'Eye of the Shepherd' was on them, calling them. But they were caught in the thorns and thickets of sin and demonic entanglement and couldn't get free. They just needed someone to take the time to help them out of their traps. They needed to be prayed for and their understanding developed.

Sometimes it's due to past hurts or perhaps poor behaviour from Christians or Christian organisations e.g. televangelists asking for money unrighteously, misinformation from family, education and media, personal demonic strongholds or cultural bondages. Sometimes they could be under some person's control or simply be of a suspicious nature.

Yet underneath they are very interested. However they have many wounds as well as lies to discern and overturn. These people are a slow burn! They need to work through blockers or misinformation they've been fed or experienced. They will take longer but, when they start 'getting it' or hit a tipping point and God starts to move, they can come quickly to Him and church.

We see this constantly in the life of Jesus, where He met with people who were not interested in church or salvation but as they encountered Him all that changed.

Everyone is different and responds differently. God will help you and them. As you listen to people they will tell you where they're at and what they need. A four-step plan for salvation doesn't always work. This is why it's important to understand it's not manipulation or domination but as servants we lead, listen, love people, and work with their openness and appetite.

My own journey is a testimony of this. At first I was completely against church and Jesus, but still felt drawn by the truth and the changed lives of my friends. In time as I worked my way through things and Christians continued to pray and visit, I began to shift until I ultimately became a Christian. I couldn't keep away from church and brought most of my friends and workmates.

> *Lord, I'm asking for wisdom and insight here. Help me with these types of people. Help me to see when they are not open to church yet are open to You. Help me connect with them and lead them through strongholds and hurts. Let me be a good advertisement for You and church and help me not be sidetracked with people that love talking and never change. Help me have a servant's heart and take time to listen and care for people.*
>
> *In Jesus' name,*
>
> *Amen*

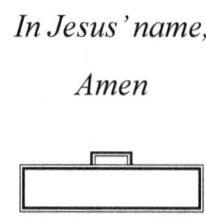

Story

THE LEADING HAND

OUR TOWN WAS CHOSEN to build the oil rig for the North Rankin Gas Project. It was a massive project. Once built, it floated on huge pontoons and had to be lowered and established on the seabed of the northwest coast of Western Australia. Later the Pipe Coating Factory was built. We had to coat the pipeline both internally (flow coat) and externally (protection from rust). At that time it was the second-longest pipeline in the world. After I was healed from the wheelchair I worked on both projects and saw what I have named many 'unbelievable' and 'beachhead' converts come to Christ.

At the Pipe Coating Plant, I was in charge of quality control across five shifts. Close to 200 people worked the five shifts. It involved getting the surfaces prepared for painting and then painting the 12 metre long pipes that were 1 metre in diameter. They were heated to extreme temperatures and then the paint was sprayed on, all done using state of the art machines.

I saw a genuine revival take place here, with many people across the five shifts becoming Christians. It was one of the most amazing times of my life.

Every shift was run by a leading hand or a shift boss. This particular leading hand was in charge of the internal preparation and painting for the flow coat side. He was a no-nonsense operator, lean, tough and very in-charge, but fair. He never backed down from a fight, wasn't intimidated and loved his beer. A true blue Aussie. (Mad Thommo got a job on his shift for a while, which was not easy for him.)

As I was in charge of quality control for the whole factory, I had to oversee both the floor and the whole operation. This meant I had the opportunity to speak to lots of people and especially the 'leading hands'.

I discovered The Leading Hand was a bit of a thinker. He was not your typical beer-and-football type of guy. He was interested in numerous topics including big picture things like world events. This made for some interesting conversations. Beyond that, he was going through some struggles with his partner. I think his love of beer might have played a role in their struggles.

Because he was a thinker I decided to give him a book. I took some time in choosing the right one, and settled on a good overview of world events in view of the Bible plus a solid application of what it was to be a Christian—but without being too hard to digest. He had very little Christian understanding, so I needed something that wasn't over the top and was down to earth. When I gave it to him he was very appreciative that I had thought of him. Sometimes, sadly, when you give a person a book it can sit on their bedside table for months without being opened.

Not this guy, he read it and returned it within a week. I have a clear memory of him handing the book back to me with a distinct shift in him. His eyes were clearer and he carried more light and hope. He said slowly with some wonderment in his voice, 'Now that was a GOOD book, it was really amazing,' and with fire in his eyes, he added, 'and challenging too.' He had not just read it but digested it and God had worked some stuff in him through it.

It was an 'aha' moment for me. Not only was he open and getting traction but also I realised the power a 'good' book had to continue to build the case when I wasn't there. Many times it could explain things better and clearer as well. I followed that book with another book and soon his partner was seeing changes in him and started to ask questions. He could answer some but others had him stumped and I had to help him.

Ultimately, she asked so many good questions he invited me around for dinner so I could talk to her. We had a great time. She was a great cook, they had lovely kids and we had some good laughs. She discovered that the Christian guy her partner was talking to wasn't a weirdo but normal. Best of all, I was able to work through a lot of her questions.

The bottom line was, she was impressed with the changes she saw taking place in her partner and her growing respect was opening her own heart to the reasons why he was changing.

As we talked, this new 'baby' was growing into a born-again Christian and as we enjoyed more dinners, more truths were brought to the table and digested by them. Soon they had taken in all that was necessary and it was time for their coming to Christ, their spiritual birth. I remember this well as it was very organic.

I was helping them understand what genuine Christianity was. I also conducted myself in such a way that helped them want to be a Christian and I was trying to bring them to a place where they knew what they were doing. The goal was to help them enter a lifelong relationship with Christ and not just for a season. Because we worked together and had dinners at their house, we had had the time and relationship to do that.

So on the day of their decision, it wasn't a light thing. I took them both to church and they gave their lives to Christ, their whole lives and with great joy and a deep desire and clear understanding of what it was they were doing. Immediately, they started to grow powerfully, attending church and becoming active members.

Not long after that he popped the question and they were married. I was privileged to be their best man. As they grew, they became instrumental in helping new people discover Christ. Being very hospitable people their house and dinner table was constantly filled with new people coming to church or with the non-Christians they were engaging. Their children also became Christians and their son ultimately went into the ministry.

The Leading Hand became the first of many in the factory to come to Christ. It was just as well he was a tough 'no nonsense' guy because as more workers became 'on fire' Christians, there was hostility in the factory. That didn't stop what God was doing, both he and the other workers won to Christ shocked their fellow workers with their 180-degree turnaround and transformations.

The great news was he stayed the course and set a great leadership example for others to follow and helped me win a real harvest in a difficult place. He and his family continue today living for God and serving His house.

⬗ Takeaway ⬗

- Don't be intimidated. He was a boss, a tough man but underneath an open and inquiring heart.
- The appropriate book. The right book builds understanding and revelation which creates a platform not just for salvation but for staying strong after becoming a Christian.
- In time, and through trial and error, I also found that people learned in different ways. Some people love reading, others love movies, others documentaries, podcasts. The key was finding out what they liked and not just giving them what I liked.

- If you have the time and relationship use them to build a strong platform for a solid decision.

 Your Thoughts

What did you realise after reading this story? What tools do you have in your library that could help a lost friend find God?

Tool

'PAUL PLANTS AND APOLLOS WATERS' IN CONTEXT

I planted, Apollos watered, but God gave the increase.

1 Corinthians 3:6 NKJV

AN IMPORTANT DYNAMIC to understand here is the 'Paul plants and Apollos waters' approach to evangelism that many people adhere to. This is when a believer witnesses to someone and then another believer sows and then another finally reaps.

There are some important things to consider here. First, in its context it is talking about ministering to the saints and not evangelism. The Corinthian Church was in a state of division over their favourite preacher. Paul is writing to tell them that both play a part—a different but important part. When you only have one voice speaking from the pulpit it's unhealthy which is why Paul teaches the need for the five-fold ministries in Ephesian 4. It's like eating from five food groups and not just one. Paul is saying to the Corinthian Church it's not a competition but a co-operation. In the churches I've pastored and been a guest speaker, I have seen high quality ministries bring health to the congregation.

This passage of Scripture however is generally applied to evangelism and it has created a thinking that all a believer needs to do is witness to an open person and move on, thus leaving the 'Baby on the Bin'.

If you witness to a person who is open, then instead of leaving them for someone else to hopefully follow them up, it's wise to complete what you and God started. In nature, a mother doesn't conceive only to pass the rest of the process to another.

This is the whole point of the 'Baby on the Bin' principle. Follow them up, be a servant to them and, if it's possible, help them all the way through to being born again. If Christians learnt to do this, I believe it would trigger amazing breakthroughs in the local church.

Please understand there is a time for 'one plants and another waters' evangelism but it is essentially done when you're not able to follow the person up due to distance, a chance meeting or a change in circumstances. I could write another two whole books on the stories of people I've met in airports, planes, trains, gyms and the like when away preaching or business or on a break, and can't follow them up with a coffee or BBQ. I become far more focused on the amount of time I have with them and the best way to utilise it. If possible, I try to set them up with someone local and able to serve them.

But the stories here and the skills set I'm seeking to help you develop are for the people around you. They're in the busyness of your life in all its moving parts. This is where you not only find the open people but the opportunities to follow up and build the baby, bringing the process to completion.

Heavenly Father, help me find the lost sheep in my own personal world and help me connect with them. Impress upon my heart to never leave an open person like the 'Baby on the Bin' vision and take the time to invest into them. Take out my selfish heart and replace it with Yours, so I can see with Your eyes and win the lost.

In Jesus' name,

Amen

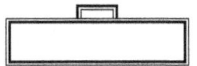

PART TWO

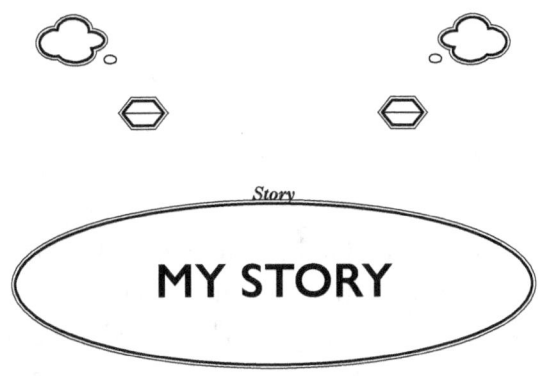

MY STORY

PREFACE

I HAVE INCLUDED MY OWN STORY here as it brings context. This section is more about those who came to me rather than my testimony because without them there is no testimony, and this is the theme of the book. Besides, many of the concepts I discuss are at play in my own story. I want to share this to show you the importance of the people who came and who kept coming back. Without venturing from their busy church life to my darkness I would have had no future and been on the wrong side of eternity.

IN THE BEGINNING

My parents were from England—Mum from Cornwall and my Dad from Twickenham, London. They met in the Channel Islands, fell in love and married. My mother was similar to Elizabeth Taylor in looks although not as striking or rich or much-married. My dad was a tall, lanky young man with a spirit of adventure. He had incredible scarring on his cheeks that came from scurvy during national service in Africa. However, due to his confidence and kindness, people quickly lost sight of it.

My Dad completed his national service in Kenya and Egypt. So preferring warmer and bigger spaces, they soon moved to Australia. They lived in Melbourne where my father worked in a bank. My sister and I were born there. An older Dutch lady would babysit me whilst my mother worked; however, when I started speaking Dutch, my mother stopped work to help me learn English. They bought an old army truck, a small caravan and toured around Australia. They cut sugar cane, gutted fish and worked many other odd jobs, and after two years they decided to set up camp in beautiful Albany in Western Australia.

My parents had an excellent marriage. It was sometimes tempestuous but they worked things through. When they came home from work they retreated to the end of the garden for a red wine and a talk about their day. It was their sacred time and we were not invited.

We grew up with limited TV and were encouraged to listen to music, read, think and question. We spent much of our time reading our set of encyclopaedias, finding the answers. Yet for all that, we weren't close. My mother and I really struggled to get on. My parents also came from an English timeframe where society encouraged little affection and affirmation.

Because of my upbringing I did well in school, including sports. But I also developed a penchant for getting into mischief. Whilst in Albany, I would climb the shark warning towers and turn on the sirens so I could watch people scamper out of the water. These boyhood antics soon led to worse things, including a police record. Due to accumulative poor behaviour my family decided to start afresh in Geraldton.

Growing Up and Self-realisation

Geraldton is a beautiful coastal town supported by the crayfish, wheat and mining industries. It was also unbelievably hot in the summer and very, very windy. We moved firstly into a very rough place called 'Beachlands' where many of my closest friends were Aboriginal. Whilst we had lots of fun, there was also a lot of fighting. I ended up taking boxing classes to survive.

I really 'grew up' at age 14, and decided small criminal behaviour would only lead me to bigger criminal behaviour. The consequences would not be worth the risk. So I started to put some real effort into studying. I was awarded the most improved student that year in a school of 1100 students. I went on to pass the next two years, gaining university entrance and being selected to study economics or psychology. I also started surfing at this time which I've done my whole life.

Sadly, around this time my mother was diagnosed with Multiple Sclerosis. This is a wicked and crippling disease and ultimately led to her untimely and early death. I saw my father manage his work and care for my mother quite heroically for many years.

Bar Work Opens Many Doors

I really couldn't afford university and found work as a cellar man in a bar until I figured out what to do with my life. The problem was this bar was the coolest in town. I was introduced to a wide range of characters and habits that, while fun at the time, didn't point me in the right direction.

After a year, my closest friend and I decided to travel around Australia, and then the world. He was a great guy and had a tender heart before God but I was the complete opposite. I hated Christianity. I'm not sure why. I read quite prolifically and especially noted the pain the church historically caused throughout the ages. I now know that wasn't the complete story. The 'real' church is something quite different. My hate, however, was far deeper than that—one year I systematically closed all the Scripture classes down in my primary school by terrorising the Scripture teachers.

As we hitch-hiked around Australia my friend would always want to talk to the people handing out flyers about Christ. I would savage them. Strangely, I became a Christian before he did. He ended up finding work in the deserts of South Australia and then went onto Queensland. I travelled to Sydney and then onto New Zealand. On the way over I became quite sick, my eyes swelled with severe conjunctivitis, and then my arm became paralysed and only freed up with several injections. Later, this would develop into something extremely debilitating.

New Zealand was the complete opposite of Western Australia, particularly Geraldton. It had mountains, rivers, green hills and no snakes or spiders that killed you. It's truly an amazingly beautiful place, especially the South Island. The Pocket Rocket from Rocky (story in book three) and I got jobs in Queenstown but we spent lots of time in Dunedin.

The Ashram and Battle for Truth

In Dunedin we lived in a Hindu ashram. Every day we meditated for half an hour then chanted for another half hour. We completed two hours of yoga a day, ate very cleanly and grew in the ways of the east quite quickly. However for me there were several conflicts. Everyone would bow down to an altar that held 'gods' on it. Something inside said it was very wrong. So when everyone in the ashram bowed down, I stood. I never bowed in the six months I lived there.

I also got into great arguments about 'God', especially when we had to still the waters of our souls so we could see who we were, and see that we were 'gods' too. I practised the things I learnt in the ashram for a year and a half very seriously. But it had no power to deliver me from bad habits. I couldn't worship or understand their 'gods' and I saw too many contrary things to give my life to it. When I became seriously sick it had no power to comfort or heal me.

The Sickness Savagely Returns

The sickness I first experienced flared up and I ended up in Auckland Hospital. When the first lot of extreme pain came it lasted several days and my knees were paralysed. I was diagnosed with Reiter's Syndrome. I spent about a month in the hospital with my legs in plaster settings. When my legs freed up enough, I travelled back home.

I had nowhere else to go but back home. So my world trip was wrapped up in two years and I returned home with nothing more than increased confusion, a deadly disease, and a bad dress sense. Once home I was immediately admitted to Geraldton Hospital and stayed there for three months. I was called the 'long termer'. I was now in a wheelchair, so this allowed me to move around the hospital and I became quite skilled. After massive amounts of drugs and injections I achieved a little more mobility and was released.

A Letter from the Gas Fields

My sister's first boyfriend was in the same year at school as me and ended up in the northwest of Australia working in gas and mining. It was while working up there that he became a Christian. He wrote explaining the experience. He said God had spoken to him to specifically pray for me and to write a letter.

I was so upset that I screwed up the letter and threw it in the corner and refused to go near it for a month. Yet as it sat there it pulsated with the power of God testifying of His reality to change lives.

Unfortunately, my remission was short-lived and I was readmitted. This time transferred to the major rehabilitation centre in Perth called Shenton Park.

SHENTON PARK—NOT FOR THE FAINT-HEARTED

This was to be my home for another four to five months. It was an education in understanding suffering. I was the youngest in the arthritic ward where many older patients were twisted beyond recognition. The car and motorbike accident section was also housed there. It dealt particularly with head and limb trauma. These people were covered in frameworks of steel with screws and wiring holding them in place.

Then there were the paraplegics, who had a special section to learn how to use wheelchairs and to help prepare them for the outside world. At the top of the pile, were the quadriplegics. Everybody talked in hushed tones, in awe of their suffering. Their rooms had large glass front walls so they could have natural light and outside views. They were also on big-armed rotating beds that constantly moved them around. This was the totality of their lives.

For any person this would be confronting. For me it was also extremely overwhelming as this was to be my future if Reiter's got worse. Each day I was taken to a hydrotherapy pool, lifted up and put in the pool by a small crane. Being in the water helped to support me and ultimately helped me walk. The extremely painful injections in my knees continued. It was a very lonely time.

This was all very frustrating at age twenty. To break the boredom and suffering of living in a hospital I would escape and slowly work my way up a very large hill in my wheelchair via the pavement, then fly down the hill at full speed using only my brakes to steer. This outburst of freedom shocked many motorists as I raced down the steep hill in my wheel chair dressed only in hospital pyjama pants.

Released to Party

Very slowly the use of my knees returned and I was released. I managed to regain my job at the tavern and I caught up on all the partying I had missed. At first it was cool, exciting and fun. Slowly it turned into confusion and I began moving deeper into darkness.

Takeaway

- Who'd ever think I could be saved? (Unbelievable convert)
- Thank God some people believed I could.
- Thank God, someone listened to God and wrote me a letter.
- Thank God a family somewhere was praying for me.

Your Thoughts

What about your testimony? How might you share it? Who can you share it with in your community?

Tool

UNDERSTANDING APPROPRIATE RESPONSES

If any of you lacks wisdom, let him ask of God, who gives to all liberally and without reproach, and it will be given to him

James 1:5 NKJV

THE CONCEPT OF appropriate responses began when I was first saved. When in hospital, my efforts at disproving the bible slowly overturned lies and my understanding grew. God had left heaven to become a man, God was Christ showing us Himself and reconciling us by His death and resurrection. This enabled me to become His son and to be freed from judgement.

For the Church this is very rudimentary, but for the unchurched who have little idea of Scripture and strongholds this is complex. When I was able to see through the murkiness of my false belief and had a clearer understanding of what was truly happening, I made an appropriate response. I repented and turned to Jesus Christ.

Thus began my journey of appropriate responses. God clearly told me to stop taking drugs. I responded appropriately and stopped. God then imparted a joy to me unbecoming to this life. He addressed my swearing and shocking blasphemy and again the appropriate response was to stop. God's response to me was again sweet nectar.

At one of the greatest crossroads of my life, after bad news, I drifted in despair. I went to a place in the hospital where I could not be interrupted and cried out to God with all my heart, an appropriate response. An inappropriate response would have been what I used to do, get drunk or high or even suiciding which I was pondering, but I chose God in that dark, alone, dreadful place. He moved so powerfully it changed the course of my life.

It was time to go to church and there were a lot of 'appropriate responses' to be learnt for someone who had never grown up or even been in a church. For example, there was singing, clapping and lifting of hands, praying, giving of finances, listening to sermons, taking some notes and responding to what was being preached. As I learnt and responded appropriately I grew and God visited and helped me.

I read the miracles of Jesus so I began to believe: an appropriate response. God responded and healed me from my wheelchair. There was a great celebration in the hospital with friends and family, an appropriate response.

Even failures need an appropriate response. It means being honest with yourself and God, not blaming others but taking responsibility. It meant repenting, getting forgiveness from God and others, giving forgiveness when others failed me.

The most appropriate response I learnt in those years was to keep getting up when knocked down and to keep going to church even when I didn't want to. I learnt the devil doesn't like losing ground, and until I had appropriate responses to his tactics by learning to use my spiritual weapons, there were some hard times.

I met a Christian woman, fell in love and the appropriate response was to marry. In time God spoke to me early one morning at a conference, 'You'll be approached to take over a church today and it's Me.' That happened and we responded appropriately.

There were sheep to feed and protect, leaders to be trained and released. Sermons for encouragement, challenge and inspiration. There were times to be bold and courageous and times to be quiet and gracious. To fight for people and let others go. These were the days of huge learning curves and all required appropriate responses, thankfully the Holy Spirit was most gracious, so too were older pastors helping guide me.

Over the years as I've pastored several churches, travelled as an evangelist and been involved in powerful moves of God, I can testify that responding appropriately in each situation and season has proven wise and borne fruit.

This is also true when dealing with seasons of betrayal, injustices, disappointments and loss. None of us are immune to those. They are never easy, but an appropriate response is even more important.

Lord Jesus, help me to understand the importance of appropriately responding to You in all situations of my life and the lives of those around me. Help me to know how to respond appropriately to the lost sheep around me and serve them correctly.

In Jesus' name,

Amen

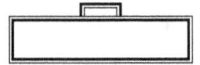

Tool

APPROPRIATE RESPONSES IN SOUL-WINNING

*To know wisdom and instruction,
To perceive the words of understanding*
Proverbs 1:2 NKJV

I'VE JUST SHARED appropriate responses about being a believer. Let's look at appropriate responses to non-believers, especially considering we are surrounded by them on every side. The appropriate response is to be like Jesus and reach out to them and not to live in isolation, intimidation or selfishly keeping only to fellow believers.

We need to be like the Good Samaritan in Luke 10 who stopped and helped, and not like those who passed by, or worse, crossed the road. Instead go to them, into their homes and hearts, be a witness, a lighthouse, a safe harbour and a pillar of truth in the land of lies.

It's also not appropriate to keep trying to witness to people who are not open, or not interested or worse toxic. I learnt that, if I persevered with them, I became too discouraged. It was like hitting my head against a wall or sowing seeds on concrete, so I ended up being nice to them but learnt to move on. Find and work with people who are responsive.

When I found the open people I worked appropriately. I talked and listened to them. I asked them questions and answered their questions. I unpacked Scripture in amounts they could handle. Sometimes it was too much too soon and sometimes not enough but I learnt as I went.

Soon a process began to emerge. Some who were very open came to Christ quickly, others more slowly. I learnt to witness in a way that built Christ into them so they would stay in the race and bear fruit.

Another appropriate response is getting the victory in your personal trials and difficulties not only for yourself but for those around you and this becomes a great advertisement for Christ.

When you display joy beyond the circumstances, inner strength, and have peace in a crisis you are a force to be reckoned with. Most people deep down want this for their own life. Beyond the veneer of telling jokes and giving you a hard time for being a Christian, they are secretly hoping you're the 'real deal' because you're the only one who seems to have any answers and behind their bluff they are facing some overwhelming challenges.

I've had people in jobs who gave me a hard time in front of fellow workers but took me aside privately and said, 'You better be right, Andrew. You're the only one with answers, so don't stuff it up for me.'

Another appropriate response is to set a good example. So when they come to Christ they have a template to follow. It's similar to a child imitating their parents. Be careful to lay down the best example so they can grow strong.

You'll be amazed at how potent an example truly is, whether good or bad. This is why Paul in his letters is always writing about following the example he's diligently set before them. He knew that, if they followed, it would lead to becoming a strong Christian. We see this in 1 Corinthians 11:1, Philippians 3:17 and 2 Timothy 1:13.

Lord, I want to and I need to learn how to respond appropriately in every area of my life but especially when dealing with unbelievers that are open to You.

In Jesus' name,

Amen

MY STORY: THE EXODUS

Darkness Continues to Creep In

I couldn't understand how I could be cool, but so empty. Be smart, but so dark. I surfed very big waves in one of the best breaks in the world. I had a host of super cool friends, worked in the coolest tavern, but a darkness slowly was creeping into my soul. Drugs and alcohol didn't help. They made things worse. I had ditched my eastern mysticism. It didn't work. I was very disappointed and disillusioned and felt let down on all fronts. But worst of all, a couple of my friends had become 'born again' Christians. This greatly irritated me. They were all radiantly happy and talking about Jesus 'this' and Jesus 'that'.

Taking Down Christianity to Find Truth

One of my neighbours and friends, a really great guy, who also loved to surf and party with us, was beginning a dark battle of the soul. This was unusual as he was a naturally happy person. In the midst of this, his older brother became a believer and he was greatly impacted as a result. He was torn.

He was in this conflicted state for some time when one night he gave into God. Radically converted, he was filled with God and literally lit up. He came to my house at 2 a.m. to tell me. He was so happy, so radiant and looked five years younger. It was amazing. He literally lit up my dark room with the glory of God.

I was not impressed. I dragged him out of the house yelling, 'Never ever use the name of Jesus in front of me.' My hostility had no effect. He was absolutely smitten, bliss-bombed by Jesus.

I committed myself to winning him back from Christianity. Normally I'd have turned him, but he had the real stuff. He had a beaming radiance and a deep joy. It was captivating. He also had extraordinary wisdom and insight beyond his years. I knew this guy well. He'd left school at year 10 and was an apprentice plumber and not a deep thinker. I kept asking, 'Where are you getting this wisdom from?'

He'd just smile and say, 'Jesus.' That would send me into dark rantings. It was an extraordinary thing to see. Watching it all unfold was not natural but supernatural. I hated saying it, but it was good.

Now, after many years of being a believer and in ministry myself, I still think the greatest and most impacting outreach is a genuinely converted sinner growing and glowing in the midst of their friends. He was a classic!

While I was very anti-Christian, truth was truth. And my friend was exposing me to a lot of truth. Truth exposes lies so, while in one way I was repelled, in another way I was drawn. It was all very confusing especially when everything I was believing in and basing my life around was being slowly unravelled as nothing but a lie.

A key moment happened when I was working in a film processing studio. An extraordinary thought came to my mind. Usually my thoughts were dark and depressing but this was alive. It pulsated with life and light. I hadn't had a thought like it before ever in my life. Later I realised it was a God thought. (A lot of believers were praying for my salvation at this time too.)

This one thought stopped me in my tracks. 'If Christianity really is true, that means everything else is false.'

For many of you reading this who have grown up in church it's not an unusual thought. You've known it your whole life but, for someone like me having no understanding of real Christianity, it was a big thought and it meant that everything I knew and believed was based in falsehood. I stored it away in my heart, quite puzzled.

My newly converted neighbour invited me to a Christian rock concert. It was the first of its kind the town had ever seen and was part of a new church opening. It was held in the old town hall and had about 200 people attending, many of whom I knew.

There were maybe 30 Christians who had travelled from Perth to help open the church. The music was amazing, not boring like I'd imagined. It was actually outstanding and totally rocked.

At the end of the music this very powerfully built red-haired American, a Vietnam Vet stood up and preached, challenging us to 'man up' and give our lives to Jesus. About 30 people responded. One side of me wanted to go down the front and see if this was indeed true and the other side just wanted to explode. Well, the latter won and I started yelling at them, 'Who invited you to our town? Who do think you are?' These were pretty hard-core Christians but even they were taken back by my ferocity. However, not for long. An Italian girl got stuck into me. I was impressed. Her courage and boldness inspired me.

I went back several days later with my neighbour to a film called The Vision by a guy called David Wilkerson. I tried to hold it in but couldn't and at the end I started yelling in anger again.

Returning to Hospital

I remember going home and being in such despair and confusion. A friend and I drove to Kalbarri, a small town north of Geraldton with an amazing surf break. That night I slept in the back of the utility work vehicle. As I went to sleep I decided to put all this 'God stuff' aside. It was far too confusing.

The next morning two very bad things happened. First, there was no surf. It was as flat as a lake—even today I've never seen it so flat. Second, and far worse, my disease had come back and it was a hundred times worse than I'd ever had it before. I was paralysed in my right arm and from my waist down. My friend drove me straight to the hospital. Any movement brought horrific pain. Just holding a piece of paper between my right thumb and index finger caused enough pain for me to nearly pass out.

A wheelchair is definitely limiting compared to walking, but you still could go places. However, with one arm now paralysed it meant getting around in my wheelchair was extremely difficult. This brought bigger battles with depression. The reality was, I was one arm away from being a quadriplegic. That was very scary, as I had seen first hand how they lived whilst in Shenton Park Rehabilitation Centre.

I also had severe conjunctivitis and was blind for up to two weeks at a time. The nurses would put this horrible cream into my eyes, it felt like molten lava, very grainy and hot, and then put big pieces of cotton gauze over my eyes and wrap a bandage around my head. I had to eat my food blind. While I missed seeing scenery, what I missed the most was reading. Reading engages the mind and all my mind could see was darkness. I found this quite difficult and was relieved when my eyes returned to normal.

The injections were as painful as ever. So with my good arm I'd grip the back of the bed with all my force to try and keep my body relaxed. I had injections in most joints including painful ones in my feet and hands as they were affected this time. But, as always, the most excruciating pain came when doctors would push giant needles deep in my knees to take out the orange, grainy solution and a long thin one to administer the cortisone.

'The Arguer' on the 3rd Floor

In the first week most of my surfing and drinking friends came to visit me. By the next week only a few came and then nearly none. Only a couple of my closest friends came when they could, but soon I was quite alone.

However, the Christians from the concert soon discovered I was in hospital and so they started to visit. As always, I was arguing back and forth. People from other churches started to come, I later found out all the churches had started to pray for the 'arguer on the 3rd floor'.

An Important Visitor

Another important person who came and saw me in hospital and who went on to become a wonderful friend was the guy from the 'Stoned Crow Wine Bar'.

He looked like a young Frank Zappa, and is one of the greatest self-taught people I know. He pulled apart his car and its engine to see how it worked and became an excellent mechanic. He later became a self-taught boat builder and helped build a number of large and prestigious boats. He was also a natural runner and, without any training, beat a highly talented field of runners to win a very difficult race called The King of the Mountain.

We previously connected a year earlier in a wine bar and had some big conversations about life and our futures. He had come out of a very heavy drug scene and was starting to venture into 'new age'. I was coming out of being heavily involved in 'new age' and starting to venture into heavier drugs. He talked me out of the drug route and I talked him out of the 'new age' route. As we sat drinking our wine in the 'Stoned Crow' in Fremantle, we were scratching our heads and asking each other, 'Gee, what are we going to do with our lives?'

He'd become a Christian, quit his job and had driven the eight hours straight to come and tell me what had happened. He was expecting me to be very excited. The poor guy was very surprised when I was extremely angry at him. But he didn't give up. He continued to come to the hospital and share Jesus. Deep down he had quite an impact. That someone like him would believe and action the Christian life to such a degree actually challenged me to think that perhaps I was not getting the full picture.

Later, he and I leased a number of houses together and had them overflowing with new converts. As young disciples we were excited to discover we could pray and see people filled with the Holy Spirit and speaking in tongues. This became our new endeavour, and we saw this happen to multitudes of people.

⬢ Takeaway ⬢

- Thank God for the people who come to the dark places to witness to those who dwell there.
- Be persistent and faith-filled.
- The Christians were patient and took the time when most people I knew and loved stopped visiting.
- Prayer is powerful. It moves the heart of God and breaks down the strongholds surrounding people's mind so God can speak words of wisdom and truth to them.

 Your Thoughts

What have you realised about your own salvation story after reading this part of my story?

Tool

INAPPROPRIATE RESPONSES IN SOUL-WINNING

For though I am free from all men, I have made myself a servant to all, that I might win the more.

1 Corinthians 9:19 NKJV

JUST AS APPROPRIATE RESPONSES are critical to learn and develop so too are inappropriate responses. It's important to identify and remedy them.

An inappropriate response is not backing up your words. Your lifestyle needs to support what you say. If not, you'll compromise your capacity to be heard. If you lie, steal, can't control your temper, gossip or treat people contemptuously, you invalidate your influence and your words have little substance. This is not about being perfect. That's impossible to do and is not the will of God. It's simply backing up what you say and if you do something wrong, which we all do, apologise. Look people right in the eye and take responsibility. Most people will admire you for it.

Another inappropriate response is silence. Yes, it's important to live an exemplary life but understand it's your words that build the understanding of who God really is and why salvation is so important. Sadly, and inappropriately, many believers are simply too silent. Jesus lived an exemplary life but He also spoke. He went out filled with the Holy Spirit and spoke. In fact, the Gospels are largely filled with the words of Christ unfolding the Kingdom of God to us backed up by His actions. We are to do the same.

People can't respond if they don't know. There is so much misinformation out there about who God is and what Christians are and do. Non-Christians need you to redefine their misunderstandings and give them an opportunity to respond. Yes, choose your time and tone wisely. And yes, use discretion and discernment especially in culturally sensitive time frames and countries—but speak. Speak.

On the other hand, sometimes it's appropriate not to speak too much, especially if you are someone who loves the sound of your own voice. In all honesty, it's not about you! It's about them. Taking the time to listen carefully, connect appropriately and provide adequate care is the key to effective communication. Also, in some situations it's appropriate not to speak, if it creates danger to yourself.

Be careful not to be 'overtly Christian' by using Christian jargon all the time and keep self-righteous pride in check. Don't 'look down your nose' at people because they're unsaved or involved in certain sins.

Don't be at war with sinners instead of winning them to Christ.

Paul says in 1 Corinthians 9:19 NKJV, *'I have made myself a servant to all that I win the more.'* He explains to the Jew that he becomes as a Jew and to those without the law, a Gentile. Basically saying he meets them where they're at. He also says to the weak he becomes weak so as to win the weak and he finishes with 1 Corinthians 9:22b–23a NKJV where he states he is willing to *'become all things to all men that I might by all means save some, now I do this for the Gospel's sake.'*

He is using his brain, he's thinking how do I communicate with maximum efficiency. A tremendous example of this is when Paul is speaking to men of Athens in Acts 17. He begins his speech explaining he had observed their objects of worship and then uses an inscription on an altar To The Unknown God as an illustration. He didn't launch into the Law or Jewish teachings in which he was an expert, but connected on their level in which they appreciated. The art of communication is to be understood as best as possible.

Jesus knew more than anyone about communication and spoke in parables so people could understand. Learning to communicate for understanding requires effort but it's crucial, not just in witnessing but in all areas of your life.

Listening attentively, even nodding indicates I'm hearing you. Often when people get it 'off their chest' they're ready to listen. You can even say when they argue or interrupt, 'Hey, I listened to you, please let me finish.'

After all this, if there is traction, it's a signpost they are someone worth working with. Appropriate responses help lost sheep grasp truth and move toward Jesus.

Heavenly Father, forgive me for my inappropriate responses and help me to hear from You and work with You more appropriately, and not only You but others also. Give me wisdom and strength, help me with boldness and quietness and, when appropriate, help me back up my words with quality actions and make me a fruitful person in my world of influence.

In Jesus' name,

Amen

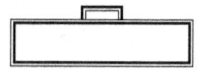

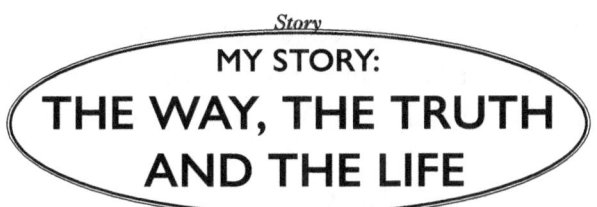

MY STORY: THE WAY, THE TRUTH AND THE LIFE

THE CHALLENGER AND THE CHALLENGED

ANOTHER KEY VISITOR WAS a former science teacher at my school. He was an American who came to Australia to teach and fell in love with the country and an Australian girl. An excellent basketball player, coach who took several teams to grand finals in our town, he was also a hippy partial to smoking weed.

He had a history of blowing up his relationships but had found a girl whom he didn't want to lose. So he needed help beyond himself. He was thinking 'new age'. However his girlfriend said, if we are going to do 'God stuff', we should at least do it the 'Christian' way. So they bought some Bibles, ventured to remote beaches to get naked, smoke dope and read. God started showing up and making His word alive. Soon they were getting their clothes on, throwing away their dope, giving their life to Jesus, getting married and were filled with Holy Spirit power.

He found out I was in hospital and arrived clean-shaved, off the dope, smiling, shining and telling me about Jesus. It so irritated me! In a fierce argument he challenged me to disprove the Bible for myself, and this is what I boldly launched myself into doing.

Let the research begin

If you came into my ward from this point forward you would find five or six books open at a time—ranging from evolution to creation, and prophecies promised and fulfilled. As the weeks turned into months, line upon line the truth was being laid out before me. The facts of creation were staggering and so many prophetic utterances had been fulfilled. I read a book called Evidence that Demands a Verdict that quite literally stunned me in its depth on mathematics and prophecy.

The Christians kept coming to see me. Many were glowing and looking so happy. One lady who had such an extra glow told me she had had an affair with a very suave handsome man who stole her heart. In the process she had lost her marriage and was in the death grip of guilt. She said Jesus took her guilt and shame and replaced it with forgiveness, peace and joy. One part of me was highly irritated. But deep down I envied her. It was something that parties, drugs and alcohol, travel or 'new age' or Hinduism never produced. Even so I pressed onward in my quest to disprove the Bible.

Out of darkness into light

At this time I had a God dream, and in the dream I was outside a door that had 'God' written on the front. People I knew who were believers would come up to the door and, as they walked past me, I would tell them about God. They would be very gracious, look at me with a smile, shake their heads and enter. A little later they would reappear from behind the door with light and peace flooding from them. I would then continue to tell them about God.

It dawned on me how stupid this was. So when no one was looking I opened the 'door' and sneaked a peek. I got the shock of my life. It's very hard to explain. It was a room with no dimension or rather the room went on forever in all directions; it was unlimited. It was a doorway into the infinity of space. I shut the door quickly, my mind spinning. What was I dealing with here? Or more importantly Who was I dealing with?

Something far BIGGER than I could ever imagine.

I was being exposed to truth and it was creating shifts in me. Many people who have grown up in Christian homes have no idea the amount of deception non-Christians are fed in their life. I was brought up by my mother believing Jesus slept with Mary Magdalene and all roads lead to God. My parents had a wide range of eclectic thinking and beliefs including humanism. As I previously mentioned, for a long time we didn't have a TV and were encouraged to read widely. This exposed me to much secular thinking. As I grew older I embraced all the new age, anti-Christian media-driven ideals circulating in my small world. These are now even more prevalent in today's society. So by the time I came to be in hospital I had assembled a maze of beliefs with absolutely no exposure to Bible truths.

As I continued to try to disprove the Scriptures, I came into constant conflict with Biblical truths. They locked horns with the machinations of my beliefs. It was like a man ploughing a brand-new field, the field is filled with all sorts of different-sized rocks just beneath the surface. He has to constantly stop and dig up the rock and then hammer out the plough and start again. It was exhausting. Truth hits lies and exposes the lie. This went on for ages, layer upon layer. Also unbeknownst to me I was engaged with the presence and reality of spiritual warfare, for the devil was not wanting to lose one of his pied pipers. However, people were in serious prayer, God was working by supernaturally 'lighting' up truths and drawing me out of the darkness into His 'marvellous' light.

Slowly, I began to let go of things like reincarnation. I embraced the truth that we are eternal—once we are born, we will live forever. I'd once agreed all religions lead to God, but now I accepted the truth is Jesus is the way, the truth and the life and no-one comes to the Father but through Him. I'd thought that we all 'Rest in Peace', but now I realised we 'all' will not. There were so many other lies I'd embraced as well. It was like the slow rise of the sun on the horizon at dawn, breaking through the darkness of the night.

Everyone comes to the Cross by different paths. Each is unique to that person. For some it's the emptiness of life, for others it's loneliness, for still others freedom from drugs or the pain of a broken heart. For me it was mainly 'the truth'. I didn't come to Christ because I was in a wheelchair or because I was bound by drugs or I couldn't hold a relationship down. All those things were true but they didn't matter or move me to salvation. Yes, we must always go through Christ yet the drivers that get us there are different. To win people we must as best we can connect with those drivers in order to present the best case for Christ.

The truths I was uncovering were staggering to me—especially that Christ was God incarnate. It was beyond belief that God would become a man. What was more extraordinary was that He willingly allowed Himself to be crucified by the very people He created so He could bring them back to Himself. Beyond that, He was returning, and the small stone would become the mountain that fills the earth and would rule the earth forever with justice. (Daniel 2)

Here I was adhering to the father of lies, (John 8:44), and had based my whole life around lies, many lies. All my beliefs and values were in contradiction to the truth of God, His word and precepts, and His people. Slowly, as the Christians kept praying for the Holy Spirit to hover over me and bring His word to life, I was experiencing truth after truth, and revelation after revelation.

It was an exclusive belief. It couldn't coexist with others. It couldn't partner or parlay. It was a narrow road, the only road. It was a war. I realised that, if you believed the Bible, you were in conflict with all other beliefs. Also, if it were true, I really had so much to lose. After gathering all the facts, I realised I was on the wrong side. But with all this truth, I still needed faith which needed to be activated so I could cross over.

⬡ Takeaway ⬡

- Without my friends telling me about their conversions and experiences I may never have been stirred to seek or wonder.
- Without the American teacher I doubt I would be a believer today. He challenged me and followed me up. Not an easy task.
- Note the journey. Becoming a believer isn't a decision but a journey that brings us to a decision.
- The power of others witnessing and praying was pivotal in both undergirding revelation from Scripture, and the imparting truths from the Holy Spirit. These enabled the roadblocks of accumulated lies to be broken up and truth to be seen, thus bringing its fruit.

 **YOUR THOUGHTS**

Who is there in your vineyard you can visit and share your testimony with? What act of kindness can you do to open the door to share Christ?

Tool

THE IMPORTANCE OF SENDING

As You sent Me into the world...
John 17:18 NKJV

THE BOOK OF REVELATION gives us insight into heaven. It's a place filled with worship, glory, majesty, righteousness, mercy, the purity of God and it's also our future home. Our home is the staggering splendour of the New Jerusalem with huge gates made of a single pearl, streets of transparent gold and foundations made with layers of gemstones. Above all, God is there, immersing it with His glory and the Lamb completely lights the entire universe. He is the sun, moon and more. Words are inadequate to describe what is in store for us.

It's hard to imagine leaving all of heaven for earth as Jesus did. He left the matchless splendour of heaven to come to earth, a place filled with impurity, moral darkness, betrayal and devils. He became limited, tempted, tired, alone and vulnerable. Why? Because we couldn't get to Him, so He came to us. Think about that—because it's profound and far-reaching. Because

God so loved the world, (you and I and those around us) He sent...

What if Jesus expected us to come to Him? What if God put on a great feast or choir of angels as an outreach for us all and those who came got to go to heaven? The reality is no one could, and that is why He came to us.

In a sense, churches should be like heaven. They're filled with the divine, with safety and the Life of God. I love good worship, inspired preaching and teaching, the rich fellowship of the saints and the grace of God which lifts, empowers and heals our soul, body and our relationships. This is why the Psalmist says in Psalm 122:1 NKJV, *'I was glad when they said to me let us go to the house of the Lord.'*

But Jesus didn't stay in heaven and yell out for us to come on up. He came out of heaven. He was sent, leaving heaven and He shone His light into the darkness and brought heaven to us. He lived amongst us and we beheld His glory. John 1:14 NKJV tells us: 'And the Word was made flesh, and dwelt among us, and we beheld His glory, the glory as of the only begotten of the Father full of grace and truth.'

Jesus came from heaven to earth and went to the people. People like Zacchaeus, as mentioned in Luke 19. Jesus went to his house and won his heart. He brought the Kingdom of Heaven to him and Zacchaeus responded. He wanted what Jesus had and all that Jesus was. This reaction happened similarly for Levi and his many friends of disrepute. It also occurred for the woman at the well and many other sinners.

I was fruitful, because I didn't wait at church for people to come to me. I went to their lives, hearts and homes letting Jesus shine. I wasn't an evangelist or someone special or even 'gifted.' To be honest I was pretty messed up and socially inept, especially in those early years. But I had met Jesus and so, when I met someone open, His burden was transferred into my heart for them.

If it weren't for some hardy souls who ventured into my hospital room, I would probably have rotted away. I was loaded with hate and false beliefs. I would never have gone to church on my own but, because the Christians kept coming and chipping away at my hard exterior, the light started to break through. One lady in particular literally radiated. She was such an advertisement for being a Christian. She later told me that coming to see me in the hospital was like wrapping your arms around a boil.

In the Parable of the Sower, the third seed lands in soil that is good and fertile, but it gets sidetracked by the distractions of the world and the deceitfulness of riches. These choke the word and consequently yield no fruit. Then suddenly life is over. In our selfishness and fear we have won no-one and we enter heaven as paupers. Be blessed, but don't let blessings rob you of the true riches—precious souls for the Kingdom.

Jesus never lost His focus or His reason for leaving heaven. For example, at the end of the first chapter in Mark's gospel, a very large crowd gathered with the setting sun and Jesus takes the time to heal and cast out devils. It's a great breakthrough. In the morning no-one can find Him, He's out alone praying. Finally Simon and the disciples find Him and let Him know the good news that everyone is looking for Him in the city.

Now to most of us and especially those who've pioneered churches this is a time to establish a thriving work, but not Jesus. He replied, 'Let us go on to the neighbouring towns so I might preach there also, for this is why I came [from the Father].' Mark 1:38 AMP

He is saying I didn't come for one local area or one church, other people deserve a chance to see, hear and experience Me too.

Can you see the largeness of God's heart here? We understand the need to establish new believers and seek our breakthroughs but Jesus is also making a strong point—that people in 'other' places deserve a chance to be healed and hear the Gospel. We must be careful not to get so caught up in our breakthroughs and blessings that we forget about others.

Here I am Lord, send me. I surrender afresh and yield to be used and sent. Help me see that the fields are white for harvest and connect me with open people in my area and use me to bring them to Yourself. Forgive me of my fear and selfishness.

In Jesus' name,

Amen

MY STORY: THE FINGER OF GOD

FINALLY, IN FAITH, I prayed a prayer to become a Christian. This led me to the three most disappointing days of my life. Nothing happened. I was expecting choruses of angels, the heavens to open up and great proclamations. After all, I had finally 'cracked' and joined God's side. There was nothing at all. Just silence.

So the following day I wheeled myself to the church next door to the hospital. I thought surely in a church there would be some connection. The journey took hours with just one arm but I eventually arrived, exhausted, covered in sweat—yet with expectation. There was still silence.

After three days God finally moved. It was in the most unexpected way. He literally tapped me on the chest with a huge transparent finger and said, 'No more drugs.'

At that stage in my life I had been drinking very heavily before being admitted to hospital. I was also smoking, taking lots of different drugs and starting to move into heavier drugs. I was being given extremely strong painkillers in the hospital due to the initial pain of Reiter's. However, I was now lying about my level of pain so I could get high. God was onto me.

But after a huge finger from God turned up and told me no more drugs, I got with the program. I obeyed. Immediately I was hit with the most extraordinary joy I had ever experienced in my life. It was so clean—not like drugs or alcohol that left confusion and dirtiness, it was rich and uplifting, it hung around for three days and I was completely set free from all those addictions in that moment.

Still no welcome into the Kingdom. Three days later, the big finger of God was back. It tapped me on the chest again. This time it said, 'No more swearing.'

Truly my language was unbelievable! The nurses gave me my medication with their fingers in their ears as blasphemy ran like a river from my lips. Again I agreed and was hit with this unbelievable joy, feeling clean with light, and delivered in a moment. I couldn't swear or blaspheme from then on.

FORGIVENESS

Soon after, I began to feel very bad about what sort of son I had been and what I had put my parents through. I arranged for a large bouquet of flowers to be sent to my parents from a local florist. It was particularly for my mother with whom I had a difficult relationship. I wrote a card asking for forgiveness. I apologised for my poor behaviour, for being such a wayward son and for causing them so much grief and heartache. On receiving the flowers my mother drove up to the hospital and wept over me. Our relationship was reconciled. It still wasn't an easy relationship but it was workable and so much better. Ultimately my mother became a believer when she faced her time of death.

Meanwhile in the ward I began to be mindful of and to care for the people in my ward, including the nurses and doctors. This change of behaviour shocked the other patients and the staff. Previously, I was a troublesome and volatile patient. Now I was being nice and caring to everyone. The doctors and nurses would look at me and shake their heads as they walked off. The other patients were just glad I'd changed and was now fitting in. To be honest they were more amazed at my changed behaviour than in my getting healed from the wheelchair a couple of months later. What they didn't understand, was I now had a new Father and I was Born Again. It was His DNA that was running through my life.

⬡ Takeaway ⬡

- It's amazing what God can do once people yield.
- God's grace is profound. I couldn't get to a church and wasn't ready for one, yet He met me in the hospital.
- I made the decisions to change and He moved.
- Have confidence that God will work.

- Your prayers, your actions, your words, your boldness and care all work and have power.
- Don't give up on the difficult ones.

 Your Thoughts

What revelation did you have about your own salvation story? Who can you pray for? Who is ready to hear your story but not ready for Church?

Tool

JESUS WAS NOT ONLY SENT, BUT HE SENDS

... I also have sent them into the world.
John 17:18 NKJV

A VERY SIMPLE PRINCIPLE is established here. Jesus is sent and Jesus sends. He calls followers, equips them and sends them. John 17:18 NKJV reminds us: *'As You sent Me into the world I also have sent them into the world'* and then in verse 20, it says: *'I do not just pray for these alone but also for those who will believe in Me through their word.'* Do you hear this? You are sent as Jesus was sent.

Matthew 4:19 NKJV says, *'Follow Me and I will make you fishers of men.' Follow Me* means two things: *Be with Me* and *be like Me. Be with Me* means I want to have a relationship with you. This is about intimacy. But it also means *be like Me* or be *transformed by Me;* it's called becoming Christlike. The fruit and the focus borne out of these is God's heartbeat.

Matthew 9:36–38 NKJV: *'...but when He saw the multitudes He was moved with compassion for them, because they were weary and scattered like sheep having no shepherd. Then He said to His disciples, "The harvest truly is plentiful but the labourers are so few. Therefore pray the Lord of the harvest sends out labourers."'*

There are now too many people for Jesus to be able to minister to them all. So in Matthew 10:1–6, He calls and sends out the twelve to minister. After the twelve have been sent and have done well Jesus then expands the scope and sends out seventy. Luke 10:1 NKJV tells us: *'After these things the Lord appointed seventy others also before His face into every city He was about to go.'*

They're sent to prepare people to receive Christ. It's also what we are personally to do in our own demographic, our vineyard, our area of influence. Interestingly, verse 17 records that *'then the seventy returned with joy'*—not discouragement or despair or hopelessness.

The greatest joy I've ever felt is working with open sinners, where the Holy Spirit is flowing through you and into them. It's very different to ministering in church. There is an extra dimension of joy and anointing, especially designed to bring breakthroughs.

This is what ought to happen in our lives. We go to church to be ministered to, and then we are sent out to serve and help others the other six days. John 20:21

NKJV says: *'So Jesus said to them again, "Peace to you! As the Father sent Me I also send you."'*

The seventy had now grown to a hundred and twenty and they were told to go out. First, as Matthew 28 records, they were sent to Jerusalem, then to Judea, then Samaria, and then to the ends of the earth.

Sadly, after Christ leaves the disciples, they become so busy and diverted they don't get to Judea or Samaria and definitely not the ends of the earth. When someone is waiting for freedom or to become a child of God and the good news never comes to them, it's tragic.

Thankfully, Cornelius' conversion opened the door to the Gentiles. Notice here, it was the enlargement of Peter's heart that was needed. The vision of *'rise and eat'* wasn't about eating new food but about enlarging his heart. The Holy Spirit was saying: look at them with new eyes, the eyes of redemption. Peter was 'sent' to Cornelius' house. Acts 10:20 NKJV tells us that the Holy Spirit directed him: *'Arise therefore and GO.'* He went and found that Cornelius was open and has had an angelic visitation and has gathered his whole household. Clearly, a beachhead convert as they all get saved, filled with the Holy Spirit and speaking in tongues in the middle of the sermon. These are the types of things that happen when you enlarge your heart and go into an open sinner's house.

A wave of persecution is another way believers are sent or inadvertently scattered. As they went, they spoke and open people responded and God moved.

Acts 11:19; 21 NKJV: *'Now those who were scattered after the persecution that arose over Stephen travelled as far as Phoenicia, Cyprus and Antioch. ...and the hand of the Lord was with them and a great number believed and turned to the Lord.'*

From this persecution and the evangelism in Antioch, God started to move. Antioch was a good healthy church that grew and became a strong centre of caring and sharing for the newly redeemed children of the Father.

Acts 13:2–4 NKJV: *'As they ministered to the Lord and fasted, the Holy Spirit said, "Separate to Me Barnabas and Saul for the work to which I have called them." Then having fasted and prayed and laid hands on them they sent them out. So, being sent out by the Holy Ghost they went...'*

The Holy Spirit is sending, the local church facilitates the sending, and it's in the 'sending' that people are reached. This is what the rest of the Book of Acts is about and we are to do likewise.

> *Here I am Lord, send me. Take the coal and touch my lips and use them for You. Enlarge my heart like Peter's and send me to places and people You are already working with, like Cornelius. Change my thinking from waiting for people to come to me and help me to go where people are in my everyday life. Work through me, let people see You and be attracted to You. Help me and deliver me from rejection*

and fear of failure. Help me not to worry about the people who are not interested in You and be concerned with the people who are and work with them. Help me to understand these people are as important to You as I am to You, if not more—as I'm safe in Your hands and Your house but these are not.

In Jesus' name,

Amen.

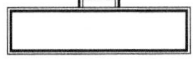

MY STORY: THE WORD
PART ONE

DURING THE SECOND MONTH after I'd asked Christ into my life I drifted into a very dark period. Remember, I was still fighting a big illness. Also, a very pretty girl who I was dating before getting sick decided to travel around Australia without me. My boss was asking if I was coming back to work. Slowly, I was being filled with doubt about becoming a Christian. The Big Finger and the joy that followed was becoming a distant memory. I also hadn't told anyone, so I had no exposure to fellowship or to church—an essential for all new believers. I was ignorant and although I didn't understand I needed fellowship, I was feeling its lack!

Many questions began to arise: 'Is this Christian thing really true?' Jesus was my trump card and, if He didn't work, then I didn't see anything else worth living for. This was not a good place to be.

The encroaching darkness was bringing hopelessness. I never learnt to talk things out with people. I felt driven to talk to someone as the darkness became intolerable. There was a very kind nurse I assumed was a Christian, and I thought she would be able to give me some advice. I wheeled up to her station and she glanced up at me from her work. She looked at me for a moment then said, 'I'm sorry, I can't help you, Andrew.'

I was amazed. I hadn't even spoken to her, yet somehow she knew I was in a very dark place and knew she couldn't help. This brought me to a great crossroad—I was angry and despairing, and was starting to spiral downwards. I was on the verge of turning my back on Christ, perhaps even suiciding.

In desperation I decided to go and have one last prayer to God. I wheeled around the ward looking for a place where I wouldn't be disturbed. I found a shower cubicle nobody used. I parked myself and began to cry out to God. It was not pretty. It was raw and real. I wasn't interested in playing games or trying to sound religious. I needed real help, guidance and light. I was going down a whirlpool.

A vision of a landscape in the distance began to emerge. It was smoky, dark and overlaid with red, and I could dimly make out people being crucified and then left on crosses. Then the scene was imparted into my heart, bypassing my mind, giving me the knowledge of the innocence of Christ, the complete and absolute innocence, the total injustice of it all.

I began to weep and I couldn't stop. Never have I wept like this before or since. I wept and wept. I rested my head on the wall of the shower and wept until there were no tears left in my body. They were soaking the wall to the floor.

Then suddenly I was sucked upwards and travelled from blackness to a brilliant light blue. I'd come to the centre of the universe. I'm not sure how I knew that. I just did. I was also filled with the most extraordinary joy I've ever known, far greater than the joy I had previously experienced after obeying the Big Finger, and far greater than anything since then. It was such a contrast to the blackness and hopelessness of the hospital.

As I looked up, two absolutely enormous three-dimensional words filled my whole vision. They were at the centre of the universe and upon them hung everything in the universe. They were extraordinarily high, long and wide. They were made from pure solid granite. I was very, very small as I stood before them.

The two words were: *THE WORD*.

I was greatly puzzled, I had no idea what that meant and had not read the Book of John yet. But I knew at the centre of everything seen and unseen was *THE WORD*—immovable, overwhelming and powerful.

As I took all this in, I was suddenly taken back to my body. I returned to my room retaining the joy of the experience, which I was very grateful for after being in such a dark place.

Takeaway

- At the greatest point of need in my life, Christ met me the most powerfully.
- When we get into these places of great difficulty, the answer is not to run away, backslide or even suicide, but to run to God and His Word. Simply be honest and look to Him for help. He is faithful.
- The Word is the centre of everything and we need to make the Word the centre of our lives.

Your Thoughts

What stories do you have from your personal life that might impact or help a lost sheep?

Tool

THE POWER OF ONE

THE PARABLE OF THE LOST SHEEP

Then all the tax collectors and the sinners drew near to Him to hear Him. And the Pharisees and scribes complained, saying, "This Man receives sinners and eats with them." So He spoke this parable to them, saying:

"What man of you, having a hundred sheep, if he loses one of them, does not leave the ninety-nine in the wilderness, and go after the one which is lost until he finds it? And when he has found it, he lays it on his shoulders, rejoicing. And when he comes home, he calls together his friends and neighbours, saying to them, 'Rejoice with me, for I have found my sheep which was lost!' I say to you that likewise there will be more joy in heaven over one sinner who repents than over ninety-nine just persons who need no repentance.

ANDREW PURCHASE

THE PARABLE OF THE LOST COIN

"Or what woman, having ten silver coins, if she loses one coin, does not light a lamp, sweep the house, and search carefully until she finds it? And when she has found it, she calls her friends and neighbours together, saying, 'Rejoice with me, for I have found the piece which I lost!' Likewise, I say to you, there is joy in the presence of the angels of God over one sinner who repents."

Luke 15:1–10 NKJV

I HAD BEEN SENT to Australia's largest city, Sydney, to take over a very small pioneer church. Everything was bigger, faster, higher and more crowded, especially the amount of people on the roads. I went from three traffic lights and everyone smiling at each other and shouting out 'hi' to three hundred thousand traffic lights and just about everyone shouting profanities with death stares.

Not long after I'd arrived, I was standing on the top level of the railway station close to my church and home. As far as I could see there were towers of flats all crammed and packed with people. As I looked at them spreading out as far as the eye could see, housing hundreds and thousands of people I was seriously overwhelmed. I uttered a small cry to God, 'How am I to reach all these people?'

He replied, 'One by One.'

We made that our motto. Everyone would win a person from their own harvest field, and we grew. We doubled, so we included the new converts in this approach and we doubled again. And while we operated as a team and did outreaches, neighbourhood healing crusades, concerts and a variety of other things, we also encouraged people to find the open people in their world and they did.

Sadly, what I've learnt is most Christians believe it's not their responsibility to win the lost but the role of the pastor or the evangelist. Many believe the lost will be won in the thousands and even millions by some sovereign move of God. Let's hope so! But in the meantime, the key is not someone else, but you and I doing the 'one by one'.

If you can win one or even two people a year or in a couple of years, helping them grow into strong Christians and getting them involved in a church, you have done well. This is what should happen when we become a believer—we bear fruit.

In the flow of life people grow up, fall in love, get married and have children. This is not for some 'special' people, some gifted people but this is mainly true for all people. Year after year, decade after decade, century after century the world continues to grow because of one simple factor—babies, and they generally come one by one. It's called bearing fruit.

God didn't speak seven billion people into existence but created Adam and Eve. They had a child and that process continued, until here we are today at seven billion people.

Similarly, when God created a nation for Himself, He began by calling one man, Abraham. He challenged him to live a surrendered life and believe Him for everything. God promised Him multitudes but it began with one child. The point is: from one comes many. Just remember God never loses sight of 'the one' and neither should we.

In the midst of Christ's training of the 3, the 12 and the 70, He was constantly making room for individuals. These make up some of the best stories of the whole Bible. The leper asking if He's willing—and He is. He goes with Jarius to heal his daughter but is interrupted by the woman with the issue of blood. She gets her miracle. He doesn't rebuke her but makes room for her and honours her. Then He continues on to raise Jairus' daughter from the dead. The Roman centurion who comes and only needs a command from Jesus, and Jesus makes room. Blind Bartimaeus is ignored by everyone—but not Jesus. The widow and her dead son at Nain are stopped and her son is brought back to life. Sometimes, Jesus even deviates from His path just to talk to someone like the woman at the well.

In the Book of Acts whilst multitudes are being saved there are also stories of the power of one. Individual stories, like the conversion of Saul or the first non-Jewish person, Cornelius. A good woman, Dorcas, is raised from the dead. A certain lady, Lydia, a seller of purple cloth is converted and so too is the keeper of a jail in Philippi.

One of the most amazing stories is that of Philip in Acts 8. He's just triggered a revival in Samaria when he's whisked away to help one person. In a rational sense, you'd stay in the midst of a revival. But God sees the heart of 'the one'—an important man of great authority, a eunuch serving Candace, Queen of Ethiopia. He's a seeker of God and truth, like Cornelius, and the Holy Spirit says to Philip: *'Go near.'*

Grasp how God is involved in the lives of the unsaved and wants to send us to connect, hear and lead them to Himself. As we've seen in Luke 15, 'the one' is so important that He left the 99, and He leaves nothing unturned until He has found the one lost coin.

Bottom line here is to realise and remember that 'the one' is very important. Don't get so lost in dreaming and believing for the thousands that you miss the one.

Lord Jesus, help me to become more fruitful. Give me a revelation of how important 'the one' is to You. Show me who the 'ones' are in my neighbourhood and personal world. Guide me to them and help me to connect with them and introduce them to You. I want to be fruitful and experience working with You to see the lost sheep found.

In Your name I pray,

Amen

MY STORY: THE WORD
PART TWO

'THE WORD' EXPERIENCE had lifted me out of depression and unbelief. I was in a better place. I was feeling happier and had started reading the New Testament again.

God speaks when you read the Bible. When He highlights a verse, He's showing you a rhema word. This means a 'specific' word rather than the Logos word, the more 'general' word. We need both. We all need constant systematic understanding of the plotline, characters, themes and the doctrines of Scripture as well as nourishes our spirit and illuminates our mind. This is so important, but we also need God to speak or spotlight a Scripture, to make it come alive and unfold it for our specific situation.

Mostly rhema words are encouraging and enriching. They have a strong dimension of peace, light and uplift. They unpack revelation and strategy. However, they can also be convicting, cutting out the bad. Sometimes they're even confronting. That was my first experience.

Because I had no Christian background and I wasn't yet in a church, I had no idea the Bible could 'come alive'. So imagine my surprise as I'm peacefully reading through the Scriptures when one of them suddenly jumped off the page and gave me an electrical shock. Perhaps a better picture would be a cartoon from Walt Disney where the Scripture turns into a baseball bat and hits me right between the eyes. That's what happened and it was a major turning point in my life. The Scripture in question was:

> *Therefore whoever confesses Me before men, him I will confess before My Father who is in heaven but whoever denies Me before men, him I will also deny before My Father who is in heaven.*
>
> Matthew 10:32–33 NKJV

God was telling me my time as a secret embarrassed believer was at an end. I needed to tell people what had happened, who Jesus really was and not hide my light under a basket (Matthew 5).

If I was now going to tell people I was a Christian, there was one very key man and family who'd played a major part in it all. So I thought it was important he should be one of the first to know. I phoned and asked him to visit the hospital as I had some news for him.

Some years earlier I'd made friends with his son when I was in Year 10. I was around 15 years old and occasionally visited their home. This nearly always ended in an invite for dinner. He was the administrator at the local Anglican Church and was a genuine Christian. At the end of dinner they'd pull out a Bible and do a thing called 'family devotions' that I always mocked. However, they held tight and would smile and answer my questions. One time they said, 'God's going to make you a preacher one day, Andrew.' I would always scoff at them but something jumped deep inside of me when they said that. It really freaked me out.

In the last year of school I had some major conflict with my mum. I had to move out. This good Christian family allowed me to stay in a caravan on their property. They showed me a strong but kind Christianity. Most importantly I got on 'their prayer list' and so did my mother. From the very first time I went to live with them they began to pray daily for my mother and me. It was seven years for me and twelve years for my mother. Interestingly, my mother and I are the ones who've become Christians in our family.

It really shows the power of prayer. My mother gave her life to Christ several years ago. As she lay in hospital about to lose her battle with MS and cancer, she told me she had watched my life as well as observed my friends who had followed me into Christianity. She could see that Jesus was real. Our changed lives had greatly impacted her. She confessed she was not ready for death and what lay before her. So I prayed with her to receive Christ. This was quite surreal as she was one of the main people who had formatted my anti-Christian beliefs and lifestyle.

Now after hearing from me, this man visited me in hospital. I explained to him all that had happened to me and thanked him for his family's patience and prayer. His response caught me by surprise. He wept.

Both my mother and I owe them so much. He was an Anglican Hitman who took us out with the power of persistent prayer, gracious strength and family devotions.

⬡ Takeaway ⬡

- The power of prayer is such an important dynamic to see other people saved. Your prayers 'avail much'. Never underestimate them and never stop praying. It might take a few days, weeks, months or even years.
- The night they prophesied I would be a preacher when I mocked them, the words went out from their mouths and didn't return void.
- Don't give up. Keep believing and keep pressing in. Hold your ground.
- The prayers of this family linked with those who kept speaking truth and with those who challenged me.
- All these things joined forces with the One who created me for the Kingdom of light.

☁ Your Thoughts ☁

Are there people in your vineyard you can start praying for?

BEACHHEADS

'Go home to your friends and tell them great things the Lord has done for you, and how He has had compassion on you.'

Mark 5:19 NKJV

THIS BOOK WAS ORIGINALLY titled *Beachheads and Unbelievable Converts* because of the great power I witnessed in both. When you grasp how powerful they are, it will open up the harvest field like nothing you have ever seen. Understanding Beachheads (Unbelievable Converts explained in next tools) is a cornerstone of the book and the reason this chapter has not appeared earlier is because several things needed to be set up first. The beachhead convert will bring breakthrough to church growth and yet for some reason it is unheard of and unheralded.

In a sense this whole book is about the story of a beachhead convert. *'From one comes many'* (Hebrews 11:12). I first saw this 'beachhead' principle play out in my own life. I won my immediate friends, then the people I knew, then my workmates and the others I met on the journey. Many of these went and did likewise. This is a Scriptural pattern in the life of Christ, the Book of Acts, as well as in the history of revivals.

A *beachhead* is a military term. The most famous beachhead happened in World War II. All Europe was under the destructive control of the Nazis. The Allies had assembled a great force of troops and machines in England— the biggest the world had ever seen to that day. The Nazis had fortified the borders under the popular strategist, General Rommel, paying extra attention to the coast of France near England. The allies launched 'D' Day on 6 June 1944, the goal being to obtain a beachhead on the shores of Normandy. From there, they had a doorway to win the rest of Europe.

In Christianity the beachhead convert is not a place but a person. They open up a whole harvest field. I could never have reached all of the Ice Man's friends. His friends saw his changed life—he went from the man who brought the fear of death, to the man who brought *'life, and life more abundantly.'* He is a beachhead convert.

Remember new converts will not know as much as you, but will have much more impact! God is at work in them and His light is shining for all to see. Yes, they will make mistakes and get Scriptures mixed up. They're brand-new Christians and that's okay. Let them shine. The new converts at the Pipe Coating Factory (stories appear in book two) were far more effective than any outreach or witnessing I could do or organise. As they shared their personal experiences they shone with the glory of God and the message was backed up by their transformations. The Pipe Coating Factory conversions were far more visual than most situations because we had 200 workers packed into a relatively small factory. Most people knew each other outside work. They became burning bushes that wouldn't go out.

The key here is understanding the power of the beachhead conversion leads to many other salvations. The Fox (Book Two) won nearly all of his extended family numbering fifty people. The Angry Biker'triggered an incredible harvest of souls in his wife's family and the entire caravan park. Mr Slow Burn (appears in Book Three) was insanely fruitful, greatly impacting his unsaved friends and family and saw large numbers of them become believers. Many of the stories in the book have this same dynamic. It seemed that when I focused on the one, the one, won many.

Obviously, the woman at the well in John 4 is an outstanding beachhead. In meeting with Jesus she brings her village to salvation. The same in the calling of Levi and his party in Luke 5:29.

The demoniac of the Gadarenes is another. In Mark 5 he is delivered from numerous and powerful demons, then Jesus commissions him as a beachhead to tell his story to the ten cities of Decapolis. Can you imagine this playing out? Everyone in the area greatly feared the demoniac and yet now he stood in his right mind before them witnessing the incredible power and reality of Christ.

The Ethiopian eunuch in Acts 8:26-40 is another. History tells us this 'one man' went back and became a beachhead convert for his nation. Ethiopia continued as a Christian country for an extraordinary period of time.

In Acts 15 Paul is summoned to Macedonia by the Holy Spirit. There God had two powerful beachheads waiting for him: Lydia and the Jailer. They brought their entire households and an instant church commenced. Just two people have brought remarkable traction for pioneering a church. That's the power of a beachhead convert.

And of course there is the story of Cornelius the first Gentile convert in Acts 10 who gathered his entire extended family. Their salvations literally created an instant church.

This is genuine growth— not transfer growth from one church to another—but rather, as Colossians 1:13 describes, people translated from the kingdom of darkness into the kingdom of light. This is the best and truest growth. This is the power of beachheads. They can cause a serious acceleration of genuine growth. They are a walking altar call. The mix of both their transformation and natural leadership skills lead many people to Christ, bringing serious breakthroughs for the churches who choose to work with them.

If individual Christians, Bible studies, cell groups and whole churches would seriously pray, fast and believe for beachheads and reach out to the non-Christians around them, their sowing will reap significant growth. Beachheads bring others. It may be 5, 50 or 500. Whatever the number, they bring others. They can't help it, they must, it's innately in them.

I remember when we had a breakthrough with our youth. We had struggled for a season and then it broke open. We had two baptismal days in two months both numbering around 35 each. After they were baptised at the local beach they all held hands and prayed together out loud, asking Him to make their lives count. It was a powerful sight.

None of them were church kids. Many were skilled sports people, ranging from high level swimmers to basketball players representing State and Australia. When I made inquiries about the source of the breakthrough, it was traced back to two people. A recently converted young woman just out of high school and a young rapper originally from PNG. They were instrumental beachheads who created a movement of new generation leaders for us in a very short period of time.

A young lady from Boston was travelling to San Francisco and stepped into a powerful church. It was experiencing revival and she encountered God. Deciding to stay, she wrote to her friends telling them to come and see what God was doing. Many of them came. They wrote to their friends and they came. Suddenly a powerful move of God took place. Nearly all these people went out to many nations preaching the Gospel—all because one girl wrote to her friends. Beachhead!

One of the reasons for the attack on new Christians is because of their capacity to influence their people group. The devil will attack a person or a ministry when it's most vulnerable, primarily in its infancy. We see this in the infancy of Moses and also Jesus. Demonic attacks were led against them to destroy them and negate their future influence.

This is one of the main reasons I take time to work closely with people. They then have strong roots to withstand the winds, and have developed discernment to protect them in spiritual warfare. I help them come to a solid decision made by their will, not just their emotions. Feelings can crack easily. Their will supports a deep desire to make their walk with God work both privately and publicly—ultimately producing fruit.

> *Help me, Father, by your Holy Spirit to find 'the ones' in my world, in my neighbourhood, my workplace and field of influence. Help me see with Your eyes and hear with Your heart. I ask You, Lord, to bring the beachhead converts to me, to protect and overshadow both of us and help me enable them to grow and reach the people of their world. Teach me and use me. I'm listening and ready and believe this with expectation.*
>
> *In Jesus' name,*
>
> *Amen.*

MY STORY: HEALED

WHEN REITER'S SYNDROME RETURNED it was a hundred times worse. I stayed this way for over six months. Treatment this time was unsuccessful and I found myself in the medical 'too hard' basket. I didn't even get to go to Shenton Park for rehabilitation. I was left in hospital with all the 'long termers' who were forgotten or too much of a problem. I was pretty desperate not to be forgotten. I wanted to live this new life.

Several things played a role in getting healed. Forgiveness was one. I realised I needed to forgive people and let go of the hurts and pain I had been carrying. This began to clear out much of the darkness within me. I also realised some things I had been involved in from my past were not good, and repented of my involvement in them.

I began to focus on the Gospels. I was inspired not only by the words of Jesus but by the extraordinary miracles that flowed constantly from Him. The thought came: 'Why not me?' It was a bold thought but I went with it. I took strength in a Scripture that said He is: *'the same yesterday, today and forever.'* Hebrews 13:8 NKJV

Forgiveness and faith began to lay a foundation for my miracle as in Mark 11:23–25.

Another important thing: I was attending church. I decided I'd go, regardless of being in a wheelchair. I went dressed in my bright orange hospital pyjamas. It never entered my mind to change into normal clothes. I was a feral hippy surfer and was excited to be going to church. I had a reason to live, to learn and to grow!

The big red-haired American pastor who'd preached at the concerts was pioneering a church. He was a Vietnam Veteran who had lost his way coming back from the war. He'd been a bikie and then found Christ. He couldn't hear properly due to a booby trap that blew up in his face and still had slivers of shrapnel embedded in his skin. There were no musicians in those pioneering days so it was just acapella, but we sang our hearts out and God would bring the glory.

Church was nothing like I thought it would be. There were no stained glass windows, no boring messages. The preaching was extraordinary, visionary and full of truth and wisdom. God Himself rested on every word. There were also powerful visiting speakers doing a series of meetings and bands from Perth doing outreach concerts. It was rough and ready but it was life-changing. I wanted my friends and family to come and experience it, so I started to share the Gospel. I became a beachhead and saw a large number of people saved.

Mr Cool, the American school teacher, who challenged me to disprove the Bible in the hospital, would pick me up in his kombi van and drive me to Church. Afterwards he'd take me to his home for lunch before dropping me back at the hospital. He lived out his new-found faith and showed me through his example the importance of what real follow-up and fellowship entailed.

But back in the hospital I had to face the reality of my paralysis. I decided to start building my faith. My healing started with small baby steps. Around twice a week I had large cortisone needles. They were very painful particularly the ones deep into the knees. If they or I moved wrongly, I'd get waves of severe pain, then break out in sweat all over my body.

I decided to believe for no pain when they next injected. I relaxed and under my breath began to thank God in faith for pain-free injections. To everyone's surprise it worked. Not one bead of sweat, not one wave of pain, nothing but an overshadowing of supernatural peace. The two male nurses doing the injections were both rattled.

'Geez, Andrew, what's going on here? You're freaking us out!' they said.

That breakthrough gave me enough leverage to begin to believe in the bigger miracle. I kept reading the Gospels over and over, building my faith and believing that *'what is impossible for man is possible for God,'* Luke 18:27 NKJV.

If He says it, He will do it.

My miracle came not long after the pain-free experience. Out of the blue my whole body freed up in a single moment! My arm completely and instantly freed up. It was so amazing! All the joints in my legs freed too. I could get out of the wheelchair. The only difficulty was a slight stiffness in the knees. I stayed in another week for observation and when they saw the change was genuine and stable, I was discharged to the great surprise of the staff and other patients. It was all so sudden. For some reason the last bit of stiffness in the knees was hard to crack. It ended up taking a couple of months of believing and fighting. But it did crack and I was able not only to walk, but run again—and, thankfully, go surfing again.

My first job was building cray pots for the crayfish boats. I worked with The Stoned Crow Wine Bar guy and we did that until the contract was finished. By then I was far stronger and fitter. We also leased a house together and we packed it out with new converts.

From there I was very fortunate to get a job as the trade assistant for the number one welder who was building an oil and gas rig. A massive rig was being constructed in our town for the North Rankin Gas project. The rig was built on its side and then floated up and lowered on the North West Shelf.

Life had begun. I was no longer desperate to survive but desperate to share with people the life-changing force of Christ. My insignificant sick life had been transformed to one of victory, meaning and healing.

However, there were some big battles I did not expect. Hospital gives you a very false sense of importance. Since I had an exotic disease, I often had teams of doctors come to talk to me. This made me feel unique. Furthermore, you get fed three times a day with three tea breaks. Then there is the administration of medicines and needles. All this is quite a lot of attention, and not a lot of work.

It makes life very much harder adjusting back into the real world. You have to work hard to pay the bills, feed and clothe yourself. There is very little attention from anyone. You realise you're not that special after all.

Thankfully, it was largely due to growing in God I realised that, in Him, I had significance. However, that took some time to develop and sink in.

Takeaway

- Faith and forgiveness lay a foundation for miracles. Read the Scriptures but particularly the life of Jesus.
- To be established you need to walk with Christ, read His Word and be involved in a good local church.
- There will be battles and difficulties that must be negotiated and overcome.

 Your Thoughts

How can I grow in my walk with Christ so I can reach others in my sphere of influence? Am I established in the word of God? Do I clearly hear the voice of Holy Spirit?

PART
THREE

Story

MY BEST FRIEND

ONE OF THE FIRST PEOPLE in my life to become a Christian after me was My Best Friend. We had first met in the last year of high school. We leased a beach cottage together but after a year of working and getting into trouble we decided to leave Geraldton on an adventure around Australia and then the world.

We left Perth and journeyed to Kalgoorlie, a town famous for its gold mining. After camping there for a week we crossed the Nullarbor Plain, a very long affair. It's called Nullarbor because it's virtually treeless desert. We caught a lift with a couple of guys whose goal was to have a beer in each pub while crossing the Nullarbor. An interesting ride. The Nullarbor is a very straight, dusty, boring stretch of road yet quite beautiful.

Several days later we had reached a key town in South Australia and were offered amazing jobs in the mines way up in the desert. I wanted to keep going as we had only just begun, but My Best Friend wanted to stay. So we parted ways. He went into the desert and later on to Queensland and I went to New Zealand for a year working in Queenstown, later living in a Hindu ashram in Dunedin.

Amazingly, we ended up coming home at the same time and, ironically, we were also in hospital together at the same time. He had been working on a scallop trawler when he stepped on a lethal stonefish and the barb went deep into his foot. The boat had to turn back with everyone expecting him to die before reaching land. Much to their amazement he lived and ended up in hospital for observation on the same floor as me.

The Anglican Hitman and his family who'd been praying for both my mother and I had also been praying for him. This explained why the stonefish poison hadn't killed him as well as the powerful God-dream he had soon after the stonefish incident.

In his dream a young Christian man was telling him how much Jesus loved him. It increasingly irritated my friend who threw the young Christian to the ground and pulled out a knife. He put it to the young Christian's heart and told him to stop or he would push in the knife. The young Christian man looked him in the eye and said he couldn't stop telling him so my friend slowly pushed the knife in. Blood began to cover his shirt. The young Christian man didn't blink but looked into my friend's eyes telling him about the love of Christ. My friend yelled for him to stop or he'd keep pushing the knife in. The young Christian man didn't stop so he pushed the knife further and further in. Blood seeped everywhere. At this point my friend woke up covered in sweat and yelling loudly.

My Best Friend was cleared to leave the hospital but kept coming back to see me. It was in this time frame I had my divine encounters with God and became transformed. Over a period of time I worked through with him all that had happened, the things I discovered trying to disprove the Bible, my deliverances and the powerful meeting I had with God.

Deep down My Best Friend was a great lover of God. Between his dream and seeing what happened to me, he wanted to give his life to Christ. However he also wrestled with a tremendous addiction to alcohol. He loved it. It had been handed down from his father, and it caused a huge inner fight. He began to come to church with me. Then he'd get very drunk, jumping on the tables at the Tarcoola Tavern, while preaching and telling everyone they needed Jesus. Apparently, he was quite a sight.

He met with the pastor who prayed with him for deliverance and he was totally set free. He in turn won a large number of his friends to Christ including all his family. He became a tremendous beachhead.

After our conversions, both his parents became Christians. They grew into powerful believers, moved down to the Southwest of Australia and became spiritual parents to many young people in a local church. Both his brothers also became Christians. One of them stayed in Geraldton, married and quickly rose to become a leader in the church we were attending. The other brother joined the Navy. Amazingly, some years later I bumped into him soon after I moved to

Sydney to pioneer a church. Incredibly, they lived just around the corner from our house. I spent time with him and his wife and soon they both became Christians and started attending our church.

⬡ Takeaway ⬡

- The power of prayer and supernatural encounters are a major key in some people's salvation.
- Some people need deliverance in order to move forward and grow once saved.
- Our family and close friends are intimately connected to us and we want them desperately to have what we have. But we can over-saturate them.
- Because so many of my friends were open, I assumed my family were too. I had to back off and live it out for them to see the changes.
- In cultures where family is very important and even sometimes controlling, it causes great distress when someone steps out of the 'family' religion. This has to be negotiated with great wisdom and firmness.
- Fortunately for My Best Friend, his family and friends responded quickly with their hearts.

Your Thoughts

If I really think about this story, how am I influencing the members of my family who are unsaved. Am I a hinderance or a witness? Am I approaching them in the right way? How can I change? What do I need to pray?

Tool
UNBELIEVABLE CONVERTS: DON'T JUDGE A BOOK BY ITS COVER

> *'Man looks at the outward appearances, but the Lord looks at the heart.'*
>
> 1 Samuel 16:7 NKJV

WINNING THE BATTLE over negative reasoning and intimidation is essential. These two things work together to thwart believers and stop them from witnessing.

First, I want to focus on negative reasoning. We see a classic example of this where God speaks clearly to Ananias to go and minister to Saul. Ananias, however, has an 'unbelievable convert' moment and is dominated more by his reasoning than God's word.

Ananias tells God that Saul is not open and why. God tells him a second time to go explaining Saul's extraordinary future.

> *Now there was in Damascus a disciple named Ananias. The Lord said to him in a vision, 'Ananias.'*
>
> *And he answered, 'Here am I, Lord.'*
>
> *And the Lord said to him, 'Get up and go to the street called Straight and ask at the house of Judas for a man of Tarsus named Saul, for behold, he is praying [there]. And he has seen in a vision a man named Ananias enter and lay his hands on him so that he might regain his sight.'*
>
> *But Ananias answered, 'Lord, I have heard many people tell about this man, especially how much evil and what great suffering he has brought on Your saints at Jerusalem. Now he is here and has authority from the high priests to put in chains all who call upon Your name.'*
>
> *But the Lord said to him, 'Go, for this man is a chosen instrument of Mine to bear My name before the Gentiles and kings and the descendants of Israel; for I will make clear to him how much he will be afflicted and must endure and suffer for My name's sake.'*
>
> *So Ananias left and went into the house.*
>
> Acts 9:10–17 NKJV

What God is doing is moving Ananias from seeing Saul as an 'unbelievable convert' to a believable convert. He is moving him from what Ananias thinks he knows from Saul's outward behaviour to what is actually going on in Saul's heart. Without this conviction Ananias can't go with confidence.

Even the great prophet Samuel battles this. In 1 Samuel 16 he is instructed to anoint the new king from the household of Jesse. He 'sees' the firstborn who is tall, strong and handsome. Obviously he must be the chosen one! God has to interrupt him and correct his thinking. *'Man looks at the outward appearances, but the Lord looks at the heart.'* 1 Samuel 16:7 NKJV

Similarly, I've fallen into the trap of thinking certain people would be really open because of outward appearances. Yet they end up being proud, hostile and closed-minded. Often the people who look the most unlikely end up being the most open, becoming powerful and fruitful converts.

One of the biggest struggles the Pharisees had with Jesus was His choice of disciples. They were the most unlikely people you'd ever choose to lead and build the New Covenant Church. The Pharisees looked like the obvious choice; they were more knowledgeable, better positioned and 'principled' people. Yet Jesus bypassed all of them and settled on His twelve. History bears witness that He was right.

However, the disciples also had their battles in this area. God had to show Peter three times to go to Cornelius' house. He had to stretch his perspective, his reasoning and heart. In Peter's rational thinking he could never witness to non-Jewish people, yet God was working beyond outward cultural circumstances to enlarge Peter's understanding.

Like Peter, our rational thinking can rob us of great moves of God that are just around the corner. If we want breakthroughs, we must deal with this attitude. One of the goals in writing this book was to help the reader identify and overcome this battle, because it's so easy to be misled by our negative reasoning as we look at people only from an outward perspective.

Mad Thommo's unexpected reaction was a big wake-up call for me. It was the beginning of my own 'Ananias' moments. God clearly impressed upon me to go over and see him. Yet, even with such a clear directive, I let outward appearances determine my reaction and unbelief. It shouldn't have been a shock since God said, 'Go.' I determined from that day on to not judge the outward appearance until I had spoken with the person. Even so, it's still a constant battle. We are governed by people's outward appearances and projections.

The Psychiatrist in Santa Monica was smart, successful and a cool man who rode a Harley Davidson and owned apartments in fashionable Scottsdale. He spoke at national conferences and on the surface had an amazing life. Below the surface he was in great inner turmoil with a broken heart. The Handsome Lonely Surfer had everything going for him by outward appearances. Handsome, strong, a gifted artist, talented surfer and yet so lonely, depressed and under conviction. The Angry Biker was a coiled spring waiting to explode and everything inside of me said, 'Move on quickly.'

Some of the most powerful converts you'll find come in disguise.

My term 'unbelievable converts' arose because negative reasoning talks us out of thinking they can be won to Christ. They're 'too lost', 'too far gone', 'too committed to other things', 'too cool', 'too beautiful', 'too together', 'too much money,' 'too wild', 'too gothic', 'too intelligent' or a hundred other things.

When the twelve leaders of the new nation of Israel were sent into the Promised Land to spy out the land they came back saying that, while the land is amazing, we 'saw' giants and walled cities. They reasoned themselves out of the victory. Only Joshua and Caleb did not succumb to negative reasoning.

In Numbers 13:30 NKJV, Caleb *'quieted the people before Moses and said, "Let us go up at once and take possession for we are well able to overcome it."'* And Joshua adds in Numbers 14:7b–9 NKJV, *'The land which we passed through to spy out is an exceedingly good land. If the Lord delights in us, then He will bring us into this land and give it to us, a land that flows with milk and honey. Only do not rebel against the Lord nor fear the people of the land, for they are our bread: their protection has departed from them and the Lord is with us. Do not fear them.'*

The point here is our sight doesn't always tell us the true story about situations or people. We need to grow in our faith and learn to see what God sees.

We also need to focus more on the inner person and what God is doing rather than letting our negative reasoning rule. As the old cliché says: 'Don't judge a book by its cover.'

Let's not be like those in Mark 6:1–6 who reasoned themselves out of great miracles and conversions. Let's not have Jesus marvel at our negative reasoning and unbelief.

> *Father, help me not to judge people by their outward appearances but rather find out what's going on in their hearts and lives. Help me not to reason myself out of witnessing to people who 'appear' not open. Help me overcome my intimidation and boldly believe what you say is possible. Help me to be obedient to Your directions so I can be used by You to find the lost.*
>
> *In Jesus' name,*
>
> *Amen*

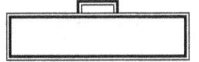

Tool
UNBELIEVABLE CONVERTS: OVERCOMING INTIMIDATION

> *'Therefore whoever confesses Me before man I will also confess before the Father, but he who denies Me before men, him will I deny before My father who is in heaven.'*
> Matthew 10:32 NKJV

NEGATIVE REASONING HAS A wicked older brother called intimidation. They work in tandem like tag-team wrestlers. If we listen, we will be taken down and not see the great things God wants to perform.

As we see in the story of Ananias, Saul is an unbelievable convert. Ananias is intimidated and refuses to go, even arguing with God's perspective and command.

Intimidation does this. It moves our faith to unbelief, and servanthood to self-preservation. It's very hard to function from this mindset.

Goliath is a tremendous symbol of an unbelievable convert. God's entire army is paralysed with intimidation because of his size and power. It takes David who is not intimidated to bring him down because David understood that it's not about appearance.

Many of the stories in this book happened because I took the time and effort to win the battle of intimidation that an unbelievable convert creates. That enabled me to come to a place where I could witness with expectation. The story, The Ice Man and later in The Pipe Coating Factory The Big Tree (you will read about him in Book Two) are examples of these encounters. The Big Tree worked at the Pipe Coating Factory and was an extremely powerful leader of men, who set his face against what God was doing. He was constantly belittling and always in your face and his aggression rallied his fellow workers. It was really intimidating but, when he ultimately fell to Christ, it stunned all the other workers.

These are easy words to write but to live them requires focus and courage. Intimidation can be overwhelming when you're on your own away from other believers. It's easy being a lion on Sunday but it's another thing to keep on being a lion at work on Monday, especially if you're the lone lion and it's a hostile environment. However, this is where God proves himself strong.

The key is to keep in the Word and keep the Word in you. Focus more on Him than your fears. Joshua is exhorted when taking over the leadership, to be strong and courageous and not to be dismayed or afraid. *'Be strong and courageous... Have I not commanded you?*

Be strong and courageous. Do not be afraid; do not be discouraged, for the Lord your God will be with you wherever you go.' Joshua 1:7,9 NKJV

Early in my walk with God He quickly wanted to establish who was going to dominate my life. Would it be the fear of man, a snare (Proverbs 29:25) or the fear of God, which is the beginning of wisdom? This became a turning point for me. However it had to be won again and again as the fear of rejection and the desire to fit in are powerful drivers in our humanity.

I think sometimes we can be 'too nice'—meaning we are concentrating on being 'good little' Christians who do everything right, so right and so good that nothing happens. We need to be careful we don't become the unprofitable servant who through his fear and playing it safe buried his talent in the earth. He was afraid and buried or hid his talent in the earth with dire consequences: *'...cast the unprofitable servant into the outer darkness where there shall be weeping and gnashing of teeth.'* Matthew 25:25 NKJV

We are called by Jesus to be salt and light. Salt preserves against rottenness, and light illuminates in the dark. We are commended by God to be both. *'You are the salt of the earth; but if the salt loses its flavour, how shall it be seasoned? It is then good for nothing but to be thrown out and trampled underfoot by men. You are the light of the world. A city that is set on a hill cannot be hidden. Nor do they light a lamp and put it under a basket, but on a lamp stand, and it gives light to all who are in the house. Let your light shine before men, that they may see your good works and glorify your Father in heaven.'* Matthew 5:13–16 NKJV

The first time I ever prayed for healing for a non-Christian, I had to overcome intimidation. I was still new in the faith and the receptionist at my job got a debilitating migraine. She was going home. I prayed for her, the migraine immediately left and she was able to keep working. She and the other workers were amazed but the bigger victory was in my heart because I saw what overcoming intimidation can do. This became a steppingstone to pray for many people over the years and see great things happen.

Remember you're not alone. The Holy Spirit is with you, but it's in the 'doing.' When 'doing', the joy comes, clarity kicks in and divine life flows out of you. The first step is always about overcoming intimidation and taking a risk.

I think this is why Jesus deliberately chose the disciples who, under pressure, chose to obey God rather than man (Acts 4). Paul too had the courage to stand against religious strongholds of the day. Peter's journey involved failure, being intimidated, buckling under pressure and denying Christ at a critical time. That had a profound effect. Sometimes it's the sting of failure that actually snaps us out of fear, regret and not pleasing God. All of these are far worse than being overcome with fear.

I was working in Commercial Real Estate between pastoring churches. As we served our customers, my business partner and I began to deal more and more with clients with multi-million dollar portfolios. These super wealthy people wanted for nothing and had the best of everything. They were super intimidating. One man asked to speak privately to me. He talked to me about a nasty separation leading to an even nastier divorce, emotional breakdown and a struggle with soul-destroying vices for comfort. I listened, ministered and prayed with him. Another tremendous lesson: people are not always how they appear.

Once I was visiting Bell's Beach, famous for hosting a surfing competition every Easter. However, this winter's day the beach was deserted and a man joined me on the viewing platform. Surprised, I recognised him as the lead singer of one of Australia's famous rock bands. He was in the middle of a very successful solo career. As we chatted he shared he was going through one of the deepest pits of his life and I was able to share about Jesus and pray for him. Another wake-up call.

I want to encourage your faith and awaken the possibility you might be reasoning people out of potential salvation. You will be surprised at who will respond and oftentimes it's the people you'd least expect. You'll never know unless you go. Have adventures, not fears.

> *Oh Lord, so many people appear to have it all together or look too scary to approach. However You know their heart, their needs, their circumstances and brokenness. Help*

me to work with Your Holy Spirit to reach the lost sheep. Let me put Your desires and needs first and be connected with Your lost children before my own fears and intimidation.

In Jesus' name,

Amen

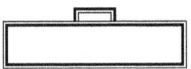

Story

THE HANDSOME LADIES' MAN & THE ANGRY MAN WITH THE WILD HAIR

THE HANDSOME LADIES' MAN

MY NEW FRIEND WHOM I MET in The Stoned Crow Wine Bar had become a believer and moved back to Geraldton. He was now coming to church with us. He was very good friends with The Angry Man with the Wild Hair.

They would both visit me in hospital with a mutual friend, The Handsome Ladies' Man. I had ironically gotten to know him earlier in the same hospital. We had been playing Australian Rules Football in the same league and he broke his leg playing footy and I had a motorbike accident. Our paths continually crossed.

Not long afterwards, I moved into a house that 'coincidentally' backed onto his. Because his was far more homely and cleaner than mine, I ended up at his cottage more often. I got to know lots of his friends including The Angry Man with the Wild Hair and a host of Catholic boys.

The Handsome Ladies' Man was a different guy to the rest of us. He came from a successful farming family out in the Midwest. They were close and he was a decent guy. We were far more feral, and often estranged from our families. He was a sharply dressed man who loved going to discos, while we loved pubs and rock'n'roll. He was Miami Vice material and we were Swamp People.

The Angry Man with the Wild Hair

The Angry Man with the Wild Hair was extremely brown and very muscular from working all day in the sun as an apprentice carpenter. His hair looked like he'd put his finger in an electric socket.

He was one angry dude. I'm not sure why, all I know he was super-sized angry. Often he'd lose his temper on the building site and throw his claw hammer as high as he could, yelling at the top of his voice. It's a miracle no one got hit in the head or injured. Sometimes, when he was really angry, he would drive his work ute down to a hard beach flat and do 'doughnuts', yelling at the top of his voice. He drove his car like Jehu— furiously. But underneath all that, he had a heart of gold.

I remembered these guys coming to see me in hospital just after God gave me the word about not being ashamed. In obedience I started to tell them everything. I explained what had happened to me and that the guy from The Stoned Crow Wine Bar was right. When I finished telling them about my encounters, it just clicked with these two guys. They got it. Suddenly, they started jumping around the hospital ward, excited that they were going to become born again.

They both gave their lives to Christ, started coming to church and grew into powerhouses. Ultimately, they went on to pastor several churches.

What was surprising was the response of The Handsome Ladies' Man. While we were all full of joy and vision, he wept and wept and wept some more. He wept at the end of every service, every week for several months. I think in essence behind the exterior of this tough guy was a very tender-hearted and kind man who loved God and righteousness and had been drawn into a world of immorality and role-playing. Realising he had grieved God, and finding the love of the Father, he was released into a season of weeping. It triggered a great healing and he became a changed man and a leader.

He didn't stay single for long. He got married to a beautiful Christian lady from Perth. While they were fruitful in winning people, they were incredible in establishing people. They were patient and very hospitable and their house was constantly filled with new converts. The church was greatly helped.

Now we were all delivered of smoking quite early except for The Angry Man with the Wild Hair. He wrestled with this for months and it became a vexing thorn in his side. He fasted and prayed and had this dream. He saw a door with *HEAVEN* written on it and opened it. There was a flight of stairs. He walked up them for a very long time. Finally he came to a magnificent pair of gates, the entrance to heaven. It was closed and had a big sign: *NO SMOKING*. He woke and quit smoking and never went back.

⬡ Takeaway ⬡

- People respond differently after salvation. The Handsome Ladies' Man wept, the Angry Man got excited. My Closest Friend wrestled alcohol for a while, the Angry Man wrestled cigarettes. But in time they were all delivered from their strongholds.
- New Christians need space and love to go through their stuff. Some people want to 'sort out' people too quickly, others never do anything to help, too scared of intruding. Wisdom is needed.
- The Holy Spirit knows each person and, when you work with Him, He will guide and give grace and skills to help work wisely with changes that take place in new believers.

☁ Your Thoughts ☁

What can I learn from these stories and how can I alter my approach so I am catering for the needs of the lost souls I'm trying to win?

Tool
GETTING ON THE SAME PAGE WITH KEY DEFINITIONS

*... I have become all things to all men,
that I might by all means save some.*

1 Corinthians 9:22 NKJV

I WANT TO LOOK AT some of the basic misinformation that non-Christians, unchurched people or religious people need to deal with as they come into a true knowledge of God, His salvation and Kingdom.

One of the most important things is getting people on the same page with key concepts and understandings. Let me explain: if you've never been exposed to surf culture, you'd think when a surfer tells you a place, person or the surf is 'fully sick', it was bad. In fact, it means awesome!

I use this example because when we say things to people like 'come to church' or 'God is like a Father' their experience or definition of church or father will probably be very different from ours. Many times it's not good. I've said this before but it needs to be said again and again. Church people can struggle to realise the unchurched have vastly different perspectives and experiences from them.

Misinformation, the devil, media, parents, friends, education systems and people's experiences have redefined key words and Bible understandings. People outside of church have a very poor, even warped, understanding of Biblical truths and concepts.

Basically, when talking to non-Christians, I'll add when appropriate, 'Maybe you were brought up with church being an old building, stained glass windows and lots of rituals. Maybe it was even a sin to smile. But when I say "church", I'm firstly talking about church being the people and a place of wonderful worship as well as riveting preaching. Ultimately and most importantly, an open heaven that brings God's grace to heal and help and I look forward to it all week.'

Can you see what I'm doing here? I'm essentially re-educating them with the proper definition as well as how church should function and finally declaring that church is good. Sometimes, depending on people's reactions, I might open it up by asking a question, 'What about you, what's been your experience?'

This always brings varied responses. Some have grown up in a more 'ritual based' church and they tend to have drifted due to the lack of relevance and boredom. The obvious pull has been the excitement of the world. Some have had little or no experience and gauge their understanding by what they've seen on television. This can be anything from Catholic services to some of the more unsavoury television evangelists manipulating folks out of money right up to documentaries on weird stuff like snake-handling churches.

I let these people share their experience and then politely try to re-define what church is Biblically. I explain it from my experience and watch for traction or the absence of it.

Some may have a good knowledge but were burnt by either the people or the organisation. To them I sincerely apologise for what has happened and I try to help them understand that, just because one church or one minister was bad, not all churches or ministers are the same.

Remember, this is done in the context of the natural flow of a conversation. I even might explain it in more detail in a later conversation if appropriate.

We not only have to redefine church but other things like God as a Father. Sadly, for a large number of people when you explain this, there is a major disconnect. Their bad experience with their own father, ranging from neglect to extreme abuse, blocks their understanding. The reality is that God the Father is in a relentless pursuit to help restore us to Himself and make us whole. That's who the Father is. His grace is there to make up the gap, or the lack, and heal the hurts. Helping people understand the true nature of Father God is very important. People who have had good fathers get God so much more easily than those who haven't. But that's what we do, we help people understand truth and we mirror that in our words and behaviour.

Ultimately, the best definition of the Father is found in Jesus. He is the complete reflection of the Father. This is the true theme of the Book of John, a major cornerstone of the New Testament. Jesus reflects the Father and brings us to the Father and then commissions us to do the same. *'So Jesus said to them again, "Peace be to you! As the Father has sent Me I also send you."'* John 20:21 NKJV

Compounding the difficulty for some people is a big disconnect with Jesus. The devil, the media, powerful people with agendas have made Jesus a swear word, a prophet, someone who slept with Mary Magdalene producing a lineage, and even the brother of satan as well as a whole host of weird and not-so-wonderful corruptions of the truth, all designed to bring Jesus down and pollute His name.

Once you truly see and understand who Jesus is and His true mission, you can never be the same. The central core of witnessing is helping people come out of the false beliefs of who Christ is so they can come into a knowledge of Him and a relationship with Him as Saviour and Lord.

Sometimes it's also important to re-define other things such as creation and evolution or speaking in tongues or whatever other things are big on their radar. Often they don't need a great deal of time, just the necessary insight that helps bring answers.

A huge thing in today's society is sex. The church has been portrayed so poorly here. The world thinks God is anti-sex. I tell people that God created sex. He designed all the pleasures of it and wants us to enjoy it and regularly—just be married. Otherwise there are unwanted babies, abortions, diseases, rape and molestation just to name a small few—all with the capacity to destroy lives. Sex done right builds healthy marriages, minds and bodies.

Another thing I often need to deal with at an appropriate time is money. It can be a big stumbling block to some people. Money is such a powerful driver and people have some very erroneous beliefs concerning it.

I help them understand some good Bible truths: God wants to bless us and He is a rewarder of those who diligently seek Him. (Hebrews 11:6) Yet while money does lots of good things, it is not to be an idol, our chief focus or strongest delight. Not only will it destroy our relationship with Him but it's a poor taskmaster. Jesus teaches us to be master over it so it doesn't master us.

I don't initiate these conversations, it comes up from their concerns. However, if it's important to them, I won't shy away from it. I find that honesty along with communication in a way they understand works powerfully. What helps is that you must have some personal convictions and insight, testimonies and good experiences on these subjects. It should not be some religious verbiage that confuses people. The

Holy Spirit always jumps on board to help you bring clarity and understanding too.

> *Heavenly Father, help me to realise when I'm talking to non-Christians, I need to take a step back and let the Holy Spirit lead and anoint. Witnessing is not about me and getting 'my doctrine' out but rather listening and allowing the truth of the Gospel to go into their hearts. Help me to speak in ways that bring understanding and life, and not confusion. Help me build into them Your definitions and understanding so they are better equipped to grow and go forward.*
>
> *In Your name, Jesus,*
>
> *Amen*

THE SHY GUY

MANY OF THE CHARACTERS in my stories have been loud, eccentric, violent and sometimes completely 'out there' but The Shy Guy was the complete opposite.

I first met The Shy Guy when we were young. Our schools had a tremendous rivalry when it came to hockey. He was a great hockey player. While I went on to play soccer, Aussie Rules and later surf, he continued to excel in hockey.

In the last years of high school he became increasingly shy. Wherever he went he looked down. In fact he was so shy he wasn't able to look anyone in the eye when talking to them. This was puzzling as he was outstanding at everything he did. He was brilliant at mathematics and science; he was a classically trained pianist and a top level hockey player. He came from a good solid family and was a really great guy. He was just shy—very very shy. Interestingly, he was the youngest child and both his siblings were very strong and powerful people. Maybe that played a part in his shyness. Or perhaps some people are just born shy. I don't know—all I knew was that it was hard for him.

I didn't see him for a couple of years as he had gone to university in Perth. Fortuitously I bumped into him during a visit back home. His parents lived next door to a family who'd recently become Christians and I was following them up. As I was leaving their house I noticed the Shy Guy in the front garden of his parent's home so I ventured over to say hi. He was shy as ever and specialising in microbiology at the University of Perth. We sat down and had a good chat.

For over an hour, I shared I had become a Christian after trying to disprove the Bible, especially in regards to prophecy and creationism. I had completed a university entrance biology exam three years ago and, to prepare for the test, I had private tutoring from a senior lecturer. Now, having spent six months getting my mind around the facts of creation, I had a solid foundational understanding of both sides of the argument.

After sharing a good solid overview of creation, I asked what he thought. Not looking me in the eye, he said, 'You're going to have to do a lot better than that, Andrew.'

I was amazed—normally that amount of information would have had a big impact on people. However, three years studying microbiology at university level does fill a person's head and their heart too. So I took a deep breath and went to another level and worked through more things and then diversified, not just the issues on evolution and creation but also other Christian truths and values that had impacted me.

Things like the reality of eternity and the fulfilment of past prophecies, even the many that were coming to pass as we spoke.

It didn't seem like I was getting much in-roads when I suddenly realised it was four o'clock in the afternoon and I had to get ready for a concert the church was putting on that evening. So I invited my shy friend to come along, not really expecting him to show up. But guess who came to the concert? Yes, my shy scientist friend.

The music was excellent and in between music sets, people shared their 'before' and 'after' stories. Explaining their life before becoming a Christian, how they met Jesus and what Jesus had done and was now doing in their life. Such real stories are always inspiring. After the concert there was a short powerful message and an invitation to welcome Christ into people's hearts. Guess who went forward? Yes, the Shy Guy gave his life to Christ. As it all wrapped up and people were saying their goodbyes, he came over to say goodbye. He shook my hand, gripping it hard and looked me right in the eye for the first time ever and tearfully said, 'Thank you, Andrew, so much for taking the time to speak to me today and for especially inviting me to tonight's concert.'

It's hard to describe the feeling I experienced, and although this happened many years ago it is still one of the most moving experiences for me. It was like heaven opened up and God shone a beam of light which radiated His love on my heart and I felt not only touched by my shy friend's happiness but my Heavenly Father's as well.

Heaven's joy as spoken of in Luke 15 was shared with me. It was a key moment on the journey and it helped me continue to work with and win people. That's important, because sometimes working with people can lead to disappointments. But this encouraged me to continue.

Let me share with you what a great beachhead convert this man became. First, when he went back to Perth he attended the church the band originated from and later became involved musically and then at a leadership level.

On my next trip to Perth, The Shy Guy arranged for us to visit his older sister and her husband, a successful businessman. He spent the afternoon explaining all the things God had done in transforming and saving his life and I backed him up and added information when necessary. It was really exciting to watch the transformation of a man of such epic shyness into such a bold and powerful witnesser. I was watching Acts 1:8 in action.

After sharing all afternoon with them we then took them to church and without hesitation both boldly answered the invitation and became Christians. They went quickly from strength to strength and ultimately went on to pastor several churches and amazingly, several years later, they took over my home church.

Then, when The Shy Guy was back in Geraldton for his holidays he witnessed to his older brother, a highly successful builder in town. His brother came to church and before the pastor finished speaking, he strode down the aisle to give his life to Christ. He then went on to play a powerful leadership role in the church.

The former Shy Guy, now My Bold Brother, went on in God using his piano skills to be part of both the worship team and the outreach bands. Touching many lives, he developed quality leadership skills, married a stunning lady and later they went to Southeast Asia as missionaries.

I particularly like this story as it shows God can work in everyone including shy, scientific people and turn them into beachheads and leaders that impact nations. There is great hope for you if you wrestle chronic shyness. God can help you and use you powerfully.

⬡ Takeaway ⬡

- Sometimes it is important to stay the extra period of time needed for that person.
- Don't assume you know more about a person than God. After wrestling with this guy all afternoon, I was surprised to see him respond and even more surprised for him to be so grateful for my spending time and witnessing to him.
- I was even more surprised that he was the key for his whole family, who were all such powerful people.

- Sometimes God does the opposite to what you think He would. His ways are different and sometimes it's the youngest and shyest who are the chosen key to reaching their family, friends and harvest field.
- 1 Corinthians 1:26–29 says that God deliberately chooses the weak, base and foolish to confound the wise, strong and noble. In fact, God deliberately cut Gideon's massive army down to just 300, so that men would not think it was them who won battles but God.
- I was pretty much one of the most messed up people in our church, there were so many more capable people: but if he can use me, imagine what He can do with you.

Your Thoughts

What did I discover from reading about The Shy Guy? How can I apply these takeaways to my own lost sheep I'm connecting with?

Tool

THE NAPKIN DIAGRAM

*For He satisfies the longing soul
and fills the hungry soul with goodness.*
Psalm 107:9 NKJV

ONE OF THE GREATEST DRIVERS for people to come to Christ is the emptiness inside. There is a place in the heart of every person created by and reserved for God Himself. People are led down many paths in the pursuit of filling this huge gaping void. They run from one thing to another trying to fill the void, sometimes picking up addictions and dark passengers along the way. I believe God is also in the pursuit of these people and involved in the process of trying to win their hearts. He is the Answer they are seeking and He is hoping they will turn to Him. That is why you are so important!

Joey Buran was a surfer who grew up on the small waves of Florida and dreamed of winning the Pipeline Masters in Hawaii, the most prestigious surfing contest in the world. In 1984 after years of dreaming, his dream became a reality. It was extremely big surf and he had to beat the best surfers in the world—in fact, several world champions. On the podium he said, 'Dreams do come true.' A huge storm rolled in, the contest scaffolding was quickly removed and the beach became deserted. Suddenly he was all alone on the beach. Surprisingly he felt extremely empty and hollow. The dream he had based his whole life on didn't fill the emptiness within him. He flew home and lost his way, until he fortunately found Christ. He is still a Christian today and a minister of the Gospel.

It took time for me to learn that things, people and travel wouldn't fill my emptiness and I also had to learn Jesus was different from religion. Lots of bad things have been done through the name of religion—sadly in Jesus' name. I knew lots of historical truth but I was ignorant of Bible truths. Jesus is the diamond covered in the excrement of bad religion and it takes a bit of digging to work through to the truth.

What an amazing surprise it was to find Psalm 107:9 NKJV: *'For He satisfies the longing soul and fills the hungry soul with goodness'* and Psalm 63:3 NKJV: *'because Your loving kindness is better than life my lips shall praise You.'*

I want to show you a very practical thing I use when the conversation turns to the emptiness of life. I've used this many times with good effect. Mostly it's been done in coffee shops and the only thing I had on hand was a napkin, so I've named this *The Napkin Diagram*.

BE THE ONE

What I do is draw a **circle** with the words *God Shaped Vacuum*; then I'll draw six to eight different shapes. For example: triangle, square, rectangle, oval, octagon, star. I then name them after the following things we chase to make us happy.

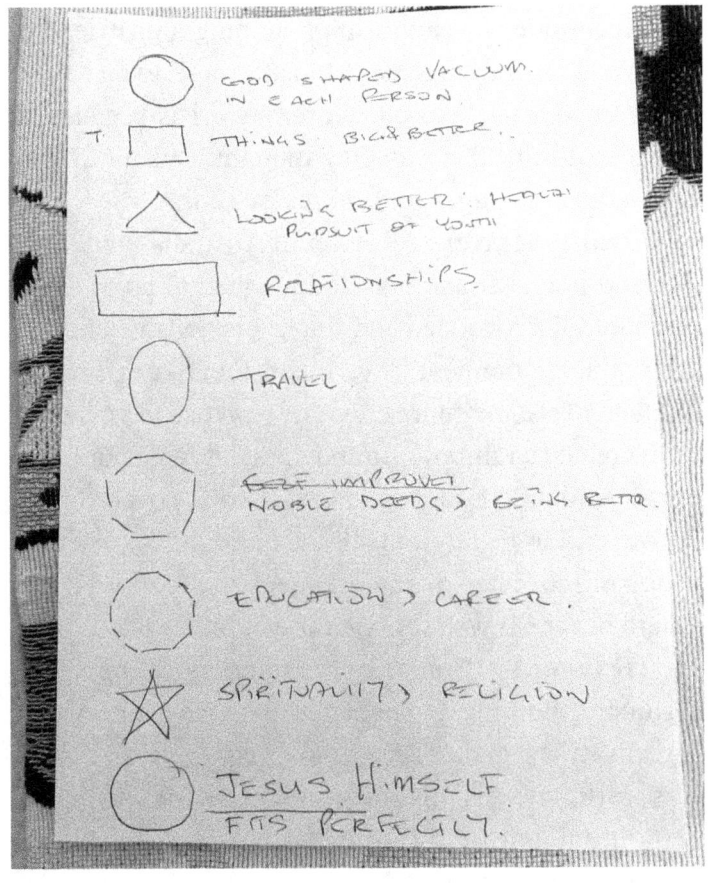

Square = Things: a bigger house, a better house, newer car, motorbike, boat, sofa or jewellery etc… We work, we save and then 'WE GET IT' and we're so happy! But the shine soon leaves, the emptiness slowly comes back and then we need a new thing and so the process begins again.

Triangle = Looking Better: being cool or sophisticated, exercising hard and eating clean; even cosmetically transforming ourselves.

Rectangle = Relationships: finding a girlfriend or boyfriend, then engagement and marriage, even having children. Years later, people are in a crisis because all this didn't fulfil them as they thought it would. Many times this is a trigger for divorce or affairs.

Oval = Travel. I'd toured Australia and New Zealand in a year and half and planned to go to South Africa, India, Morocco and Canary Islands when I had a surprising 'moment.' We hiked mountains in New Zealand to see the sunrise. As the sun rose from behind us, it created a rainbow around the shadow of our heads on the mountains opposite us. It was extraordinary. However, the beauty outside of me didn't impact the inside of me. I had a 'aha' moment and realised travel would never fill what I hoped it would.

Hexagon = Being Better: serving others less fortunate, helping orphanages in Africa or joining organisations that serve in hospitals or assist those less fortunate. Whilst a good goal and brings a certain amount of fulfilment it is unable to fill the God-shaped vacuum.

Octagon = Studying, education and career. People invest much time and effort, much vision and hope. It's good to have an education and a trade but it's not the filler of your longing soul.

Star = Spirituality e.g eastern mysticism, new age or the western religious church.

Most of these things aren't bad and, in their rightful place, they are very good. But they're not designed to fill the God-shaped vacuum or be the chief thing in our lives.

When I'm drawing out the shapes and explaining these things that we use to fill the emptiness, I'm mindful of whom I am talking with and relate the diagrams to them.

It isn't a rigid diagram. It's flexible with stories and testimonies you have that will relate to whom you're dealing with. In the end what matters is they understand that things, pleasure, people and religion will not fill the space God has created for Himself, only He can do that.

Obviously, Christ—and only Christ—can fill the circle. Remember I began with a circle called the God-shaped Vacuum. Take the time here to explain why Jesus fills this space. Explain who He is. What He has done. How does He fill the space? The Parable of the Lost Son is good to share. He gives us peace, love, protection, hope and purpose. Importantly tell them your story. Explain how you discovered Jesus and how you are now satisfied. Your testimony will bring an anointing and help them understand how powerful encountering Christ is for everyone.

Oh Lord, I know what it feels like to have an empty heart and am so grateful my heart is now filled with Your love and grace. I want to help others fill their hearts with You. Nothing else fills this space but You. Help me locate the lost sheep in my world and connect with them so one day I might be able to sit down and explain the God-shaped Vacuum and their hearts will be filled with You. Thank You for showing me how I can do this.

In Jesus' Name,

Amen

Story

THE ITALIAN CATHOLIC HIPPIE

I MET THE Young Italian Catholic Hippie during the early days of my salvation. She had just left school and wanted to experience all that life could offer. Many young people are extremely vulnerable at this age. We know this because we see our world littered with their broken hearts, and their lives bound by philosophies and pleasures they embraced early on. I also know this because I went down the same path, chasing things to make me wise, cool, and give me pleasure. But I ended up in confusion, darkness and bondage. I also plus gained some toxic demonic hitchhikers along the way as I was sucked into their fraudulent deadly web.

The Italian Catholic Hippie was very much in the same shiny web about to be preyed upon by the world. She had just done her University Entrance Exam and was smart, creative, attractive and feeling her freedom. There was a youthful spring in her step, an exciting future ahead and worlds to be conquered. Many of us remember that feeling well.

I first met her when shopping for some products in our local health food store. She was working there and was dressed in colourful surf hippie fashions from Bali. We got talking about the meaning of life and I shared about becoming a Christian. She was open and interested. Not an alluvial gold nugget (see tools in book two) but definitely worth going back and doing some digging to seek the deeper gold.

She had a great sense of humour, was a seeker of truth and a questioner of life, so over a few weeks we worked through several topics including the insidious nature of what seemed lovely but was deadly. She had spent twelve years going to a serious Catholic college and was not only burnt out from it but knew how empty Catholicism was. She was leaving her Catholic roots and starting to buy into the new age movement. This was one of the reasons she was working at the health food store.

I had to explain that the new age movement she was aiming for wouldn't bring her satisfaction. She needed to come out from a counterfeit to real Christianity, and also needed a vital relationship with Christ, not lots of rituals and rules.

As I explained my experiences with the new age movement and what real Christianity was, it began to impact her. Traction started to develop in her heart and mind. We had a number of conversations and ultimately it was the truth and the genuine love of God, not religion, she was interested in. Through our discussions she became a Christian, is going strong today, and is still a friend.

Over the next year she became a faithful member of the church. Jesus was very much her best friend and she shared what she was experiencing with her little sister, who responded and became a Christian as well. Her sister grew solidly and went on to marry The Angry Man with the Wild Hair. They developed an excellent marriage and went on to pioneer a church, rescued another and now are the associate pastors helping many hundreds of people. They have developed a ministry in marriage restoration and breakthroughs.

The Italian Catholic Hippy went to university and became a teacher and an excellent one at that and later a writer. She has inspired many people with her insight and overcoming capacity through her intimate walk with God, seeing His great hand of grace and favour help her through life.

⬖ Takeaway ⬖

- This is a prime example of The Baby on the Bin in operation.
- This is shows the importance of going back. This lady would never have come to church or allowed me to pray in our initial meetings. Yet she had a seeker's heart, she just needed time to work through her questions.
- She needed time to develop an understanding of the genuine Gospel and kingdom truths. I built these

for her by answering her questions and chipping away at her misconceptions.

- This allowed her to make a serious and lifelong commitment and she went on to win her sister in a similar fashion.

Your Thoughts

Are there any people in the stores I shop open to the gospel? Can I apply these takeaways to my vineyard?

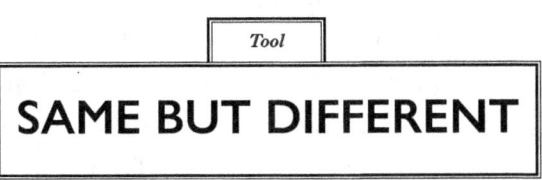

Tool

SAME BUT DIFFERENT

And have redeemed us to God by Your blood.
Out of every tribe and tongue and people
and nation ...

Revelation 5:9 NKJV

UNDERNEATH SELFIES, AWESOME social media presentations, beauty and wealth, fame and power, people are still people. We all have our battles: seasons of loneliness, guilt, fear, destructive habits, depression, sickness and family strongholds. This is not only in Australia but worldwide, and sadly it's getting worse.

When I first began my journey as a Christian, my reference points came from a country town. After discipleship and leadership training for eight years, I went to Australia's largest and most diverse city and began to meet immigrants from many different nationalities. I was intrigued and fascinated. My friendships and our church reflected this connection.

As my church began growing, I was invited to minister in Mindanao, the largest island of the Philippines. While I was exposed to God moving in a greater dimension, I was also amazed at the cultural differences. The Filipinos lived on so little yet were happy, respectful, well-presented and humble. This was in great contrast to Australian culture.

Later, I preached in Zimbabwe and Zambia—dangerous places at the time. There were beautiful people and again such cultural differences. In time I was able to minister all over the USA. My eyes were opened to the Hispanic people and their strong family culture. I also had an incredible connection and great fruitfulness with the Navajo Nation and their neighbours the Hopis. This bond came from growing up with Aboriginal friends in my youth.

God has taken me on a journey of diverse cultures, introducing me to skin colours, languages, foods, music, customs and clothes all very different from my own.

I discovered, however, we are also very much the same. We are all children of Adam and Eve, all stained with their sin and their curse. It's been handed down to us without exception. We are all sinners, great and small, rich and poor. We all have the Adamic nature that separates us from God. Our passion and focus is only for ourselves. We are all proud and selfish. We all carry guilt and shame—some more than others. We have all failed God, hurt others and defiled ourselves. We battle being misunderstood.

All of us long for love and significance. We treasure moments of validation. All over the world single people worry about getting married and struggle with the fear of being lonely. And all over the world married people worry about their children, their future and their relationships.

Every person has battles, and the burden of the demonic realm inflicted upon them. In every culture people are dealing with broken hearts, self-hate and depression. Every culture has habits that bind its people—whether it's pornography, drugs, alcohol, gambling or domestic violence and sexual abuse. Sickness is everywhere and it's more than just a broken body, it's broken hearts and spirits, relationships and families. I've done many healing crusades both in the West and in the Third World. People are broken, desperate and dying—regardless of culture, fame or fortune. We cannot escape death.

Death cannot be cheated. Life might be prolonged with medications, miracle herbs and potions and even Godly miracles. You might offset ageing with money, botox and expensive remedies but, in the end, nobody escapes. Nobody.

The good news is the Gospel works and, amazingly, works for every person. I've learnt regardless of language, colour or class the Gospel works. It works across all barriers. It brings restoration, its' a healing balm. Christ by God's grace has the capacity to help every person in everything and through everything.

He is not only the Satisfier of the longing soul but the Restorer of our souls. He's the Destroyer of guilt and shame and the Breaker of our chains. He gives us peace with God, and peace in our souls even in our wildest storms. He brings light in our darkness and comfort in bereavement. He brings joy in our hearts like a medicine. He gives us charge over devils. Agents of terror and their defilements are banished by His name and blood. His blood pays the price to forgive and cleanse. It purchases us to bring us into the love of the Father and the companionship of the Holy Spirit. He lifts the downtrodden so they sit with princes. He humbles the proud, delivering them from their greatest enemy—themselves. He leads with His Truth, His Spirit, the Word and Church—the Pillar of Truth, keeping us from the lies of deception. He gifts the ungifted and beautifies the ordinary. He brightens the eyes and quickens the step and prepares a feast in the midst of our enemies.

He is the Friend that sticks closer than a brother and listens while you pour out your heart again and again. He gives us strength in our weariness and enables us to love and lead our families beyond our human capabilities. He works all things for our good, even the bad and ugly stuff.

There's so much more, but the ultimate prize is He confronts death and our deserved judgement. He leads us through death's door, even in its suffering. He brings us into Heaven, our true and lasting home where He has prepared mansions for His bride. Us.

In a meeting in Malaysia, God gave me a word of knowledge that there was a young lady who had unbearable back pain, and she immediately came forward. She had not been able to sleep more than an hour or so a night for four years. She was beyond exhausted. As she lay on her bed, God spoke to her and said, 'Get up and go to the church, I'm going to heal you.'

She came forward and I laid hands on her. Suddenly, she began to manifest a number of extraordinary demonic postures quite impossible for a normal person. I wasn't getting a breakthrough and desperately prayed under my breath for God's help. He said it was a Kundalini spirit inherited by cultural worship from her parents. I commanded it to be broken and to come out in Jesus' name. The young lady regained her senses and was completely healed. She later wrote me a letter explaining the whole story and testifying that she was still completely healed. She had no pain, sleeping well and all the exhaustion had left.

This is the Gospel in operation. These are the things that make it all worthwhile and this is why the devil hates Christians as they bring deliverance, healing and salvation.

This is one of many stories I've seen over and over again. Jesus comes into people's suffering, bringing change, freedom from pain, guilt and shame. He brings deep companionship and comfort through difficult times regardless of whether you are in America, Africa, Asia, Europe, Australia or anywhere in the world. I have witnessed countless miracles—healing of a blind eye in Port Hedland, Parkinson's disease in San Diego, AIDs in London, the broken hearted everywhere, the fearful, the guilty, the suicidal sound guy in Albany, New York, the deaf daughter in Las Vegas and cerebral palsy in Tasmania. There have been countless others all transformed by the touch of Jesus. The point I'm making here is that these people are from different countries and cultures, yet all of them had struggles that Jesus healed and helped.

I've found that when people know you're a safe person, a person they can trust, who is genuine, they will let you into their battles and hurt. When they let you in, you simply bring them to Jesus who then loves them completely.

So don't be caught out by different cultures, classes and colour, because underneath we all bleed red blood and we all have very real struggles. Thankfully Jesus is a genuine solution to those problems. Have boldness in who He is and what He can do for people especially when they are hungry and humble —follow them up!

Lord, Oh Lord, You are the answer for the world and all its sufferings. I want to work with You to be an answer for this world. Help me help your lost sheep and lead them to You. Help me share what I have through Your divine power and be a light in their dark world. Change my stony heart into a heart of flesh that has compassion on Your lost children.

In Jesus' name,

Amen

FINAL THOUGHTS

Well, you have just digested the entrée, *Be The One*. I hope you have enjoyed it and it has inspired you to rethink your role in winning the lost sheep in your own neighbourhoods, work places and spheres of influence.

I hope my personal story has showed you the importance of leaving the ninety-nine and finding the one that is lost. For without those hardy souls who went to the hospital to seek me out I would have gone to hell and the love of God would not have brought me out of the dark into His marvellous light, along with the hundreds of souls won in the ensuing weeks, months and years after my salvation. I hope you have had a fresh revelation of how important the other six days of the week are in the Christian calendar.

I would also like to encourage you to follow through, write down, think through, perhaps work with another person even a connect group so you can implant and energise the principles of this first book. The problem is its so easy to consume a book or a sermon and then move on without it going down into our heart, as in Luke 9:44 and Psalm 1. This is what changes us and thus impacts others.

Remember, this body of work is a trilogy, and you have just read *Be The One*. This is just a foretaste of the following books, *Who Wins the One* and *For The One* which will be released in the coming months.

The next book, *Who Wins the One* is the main meal and is filled with more inspirational stories including going back to my high school and preaching the gospel; a mini revival in a pipe coating factory; and even a stop work meeting where an entire oil rig strikes over the name of Jesus. You will read of a bikie who gets saved reading the book of Revelation and then wins the whole caravan park where he resides. But while the stories are entertaining, the tools delve deeper into the practicalities of how to see the lost sheep found. These tools explore concepts like mining and fishing. I discuss how to mine the types of gold found when seeking the lost. *Fishing* is commonly referred to when winning the lost but I just don't talk about how to fish but the types of bait needed and how to effectively reel different fish into the boat, helping them make informed and strong decisions to follow Christ. I also kick over a few sacred cows that hinder fruitfulness. This will free people up and enable them to fall in love with soul winning again. There is something for everyone and a lot of ways to effect your community, find the lost sheep and work more deeply with Holy Spirit.

These skills or tools have a wide range of application. Not only are they good for winning souls but they also offer a body of wisdom on how to better work with people in general. This firstly includes establishing new people in Christ, but also helps with Christian leadership and working with people in all areas of our life. For example if you're a manager or sales person involved in customer service there is a host of insights to be gleaned.

The next book is littered with diamonds from years of working at the coal face and then years of finding the wordings to help the reader apply the insights to their own life. That's the purpose here, to not just inspire you, but help you win the lost sheep. To help you deliver people from all different strongholds, from the religious to the demonic. But most of all to up skill the every day believer for the great harvest.

Be The One is only the beginning. You've only just started. Come join me on this journey of discovering how to win the lost in Book Two, *Who Wins The One*.

ABOUT THE AUTHOR

Andrew Purchase is a grower of people, lover of Haidie, great coffee, motorcycles, big surf and interesting people. He came from the dark side at 20 years old after disproving the Bible in hospital. Failing this, he discovered he was on the wrong side and became a lover of the things of God. He went on to win hundreds to Christ, travelling through 24 different countries and seeing the lost won, healed and delivered. He has pastored three churches and continues to this day to win the lost.

Andrew and Haidie Purchase live in New South Wales and travel the country teaching and living *Be the One*. They are focused on upskilling people, churches and business leaders to be effective influencers in their harvest field.

www.ingramcontent.com/pod-product-compliance
Lightning Source LLC
Chambersburg PA
CBHW071957070526
44583CB00015B/1233